Economic Integration in Asia and India

Other books by IDE-JETRO

INDUSTRIAL CLUSTERS IN ASIA
Akifumi Kuchiki and Masatsugu Tsuji (*editors*)

SPATIAL STRUCTURE AND REGIONAL DEVELOPMENT IN CHINA
Nobuhiro Okamoto and Takeo Ihara (*editors*)

GENDER AND DEVELOPMENT
The Japanese Experience in Comparative Perspective
Mayumi Murayama (*editor*)

EAST ASIA'S DE FACTO ECONOMIC INTEGRATION
Daisuke Hiratsuka (*editor*)

RECOVERING FINANCIAL SYSTEMS
China and Asian Transition Economies
Mariko Watanabe (*editor*)

DEVELOPMENT OF ENVIRONMENTAL POLICY IN JAPAN AND ASIAN COUNTRIES
Tadayashi Terao and Kenji Otsuka (*editors*)

REGIONAL INTEGRATION IN EAST ASIA
From the Viewpoint of Spatial Economics
Masahisa Fujita (*editor*)

NEW DEVELOPMENTS OF THE EXCHANGE RATE REGIMES IN DEVELOPING COUNTRIES
Hisayuki Mitsuo (*editor*)

Economic Integration in Asia and India

Edited by
Masahisa Fujita

palgrave
macmillan

IDE-JETRO

First published 2008 by
PALGRAVE MACMILLAN
Houndmills, Basingstoke, Hampshire RG21 6XS and
175 Fifth Avenue, New York, N.Y. 10010
Companies and representatives throughout the world

PALGRAVE MACMILLAN is the global academic imprint of the Palgrave Macmillan division of St. Martin's Press, LLC and of Palgrave Macmillan Ltd. Macmillan® is a registered trademark in the United States, United Kingdom and other countries. Palgrave is a registered trademark in the European Union and other countries.

ISBN-13:978-0-230-52085-1
ISBN-10:0-230-52085-5

This book is printed on paper suitable for recycling and made from fully managed and sustained forest sources. Logging, pulping and manufacturing processes are expected to conform to the environmental regulations of the country of origin.

A catalogue record for this book is available from the British Library.

Library of Congress Cataloging-in-Publication Data
Economic integration in Asia and India/edited by Masahisa Fujita. pcm. Includes bibliographical references and index.
ISBN 0–230–52085–5(alk. paper) 1. India—Foreign economic relations—Asia. 2.
Asia—Foreign economic relations—India.3. Asia—Economic integration.
I. Fujita, Masahisa. HF1590.15.A78E36 2007 337.1'5—dc22 2007017071

10 9 8 7 6 5 4 3 2 1
17 16 15 14 13 12 11 10 09 08

Printed and bound in Great Britain by
Antony Rowe Ltd. Chippenham and Eastbourne

Contents

List of Tables

List of Figures

Preface

This book is an outcome of the international symposium on 'Economic Integration in Asia and India', held at the Keidanren Hall in Tokyo, 8 December 2005. The symposium was organized by the Institute of Developing Economies at the Japan External Trade Organization (JETRO), Asahi Shimbun and the World Bank. The symposium specifically focused on how Asian countries would be affected by India's participation in economic integration, how India itself would be affected domestically in this process, and, finally, how the regions could successfully pave the way towards economic integration.

Chapter 1 presents a keynote lecture on Indian growth given by Professor Jagdish Bhagwati of Columbia University. In Chapter 2 economic integration in East Asia is discussed by Homi Kharas, in cooperation with Enrique Aldaz-Carroll and Sjamsu Rahardja of the World Bank. In Chapters 3 to 5 the relationship between India and each country from the perspectives of China, Thailand and Japan respectively is discussed by Zhang Yuyan, Chularat Suteethorn and Shuji Uchikawa. In Chapter 6 the problems of India's agriculture are discussed by Ramesh Chand, while Chapter 7 presents a summary of the panel discussion session.

The editor would like to thank Asahi Shimbun and the World Bank for their enthusiastic support as cosponsors of the symposium, as well as the keynote speaker and panel discussants for making this highly successful symposium possible, and for agreeing to contribute papers for this volume.

MASAHISA FUJITA

Notes on the Contributors

Enrique Aldaz-Carroll is a World Bank economist presently based in Indonesia, and has written papers on export competitiveness, regional trade integration, technological upgrading of exports, product standards and poverty. He has worked as a consultant for, among others, the United Nations. He holds a Master in Economics (London School of Economics and Political Science and a PhD in Economics (Institute of Development Studies, Sussex University).

Jagdish Bhagwati is University Professor, Economics and Law, at Columbia University and Senior Fellow in International Economics at the Council on Foreign Relations. He was Economic Policy Adviser to the Director General of GATT and also served as Special Adviser to the UN on Globalization and External Adviser to the Director General, WTO. Currently, he is a member of UN Secretary General Kofi Annan's Advisory Group on the NEPAD process in Africa. Five volumes of his scientific writings and two of his public policy essays have been published by MIT Press. The recipient of six festschrifts in his honour, he has also received several prizes and honorary degrees. Professor Bhagwati's latest book *In Defense of Globalization* was published by Oxford University Press in 2004 to worldwide acclaim.

Ramesh Chand is ICAR National Professor at the National Centre for Agricultural Economics and Policy Research, New Delhi, India. He was Visiting Professor at the University of Wollongong, New South Wales, Australia (2000); and Visiting Fellow at the Institute of Developing Economies, Chiba, Japan (2003). Dr Chand has published six books and 60 research papers on themes related to agricultural growth and development, food policy and international trade.

Masahisa Fujita is President of the Research Institute of Economy, Trade and Industry, Japan, Professor of Konan University and Adjunct Professor of the Institute of Economic Research, Kyoto University. He gained his PhD from the University of Pennsylvania in 1972 and has taught at the University of Pennsylvania and Kyoto University. He was President of the Institute of Developing Economies, JETRO, from October 2003 to April 2007.

Homi Kharas is currently a Visiting Fellow at the Wolfensohn Center for Development at the Brookings Institution in Washington, DC. He was the Chief Economist of the East Asia and Pacific Region of the World Bank and Director of the region's Poverty Reduction and Economic Management Department from 1999–2007 and has been following East Asian economies since 1982. He joined the World Bank in 1980 and has worked in the Research Department, the Latin America and Caribbean region, and the Economic Policy Department. From 1990 to 1991, he worked as a Senior Partner with Jeffrey D. Sachs and Associates, advising countries in East/Central Europe and the Soviet Union on transition issues. He completed his PhD in economics at Harvard University and his undergraduate studies at the University of Cambridge. He has published widely in the areas of external debt and developing countries' foreign borrowing and fiscal risks and contingent liabilities.

Sjamsu Rahardja is an economist for the World Bank Office in Jakarta, Indonesia, and was a visiting fellow at the Peterson Institute for International Economics. His research areas include subsidies and insurance offerings by firms, corporate regulation and financing constraints, and the effect of international firm's productivity. He received his PhD in economics from Georgetown University.

Chularat Suteethorn, a Thai national, presently serves as Deputy Director-General of the Fiscal Policy Office, Ministry of Finance, Thailand. Previously, she served as Bureau Director of the Bureau of International and Macroeconomic Policy. She gained her Bachelor's Degree in Economics from Kasetsart University, Bangkok and a Master of Development Studies on Economic Policy and Planning from the Institute of Social Studies, the Netherlands. She joined the Ministry of Finance as an Economist in 1977. She was nominated by the Minster of Finance of Thailand to work as Economic Officer at the ASEAN Secretariat in Jakarta during 1983–88. She serves as a resource person on economic cooperation under the ASEAN Committee on Finance and Banking, with experience at the ASEAN Free Trade Area.

Shuji Uchikawa is Senior Researcher, Bangkok Research Center, JETRO. He gained his PhD from Jawaharlal Nehru University in 1994, and has taught as a Lecturer in the Faculty of Administration and Informatics, Tokoha-gakuen Hamamatsu University in 1993–96 and was a Visiting Faculty Member of the Indira Gandhi Institute of Development Research, Mumbai in 2000–02.

Zhang Yuyan is Deputy Director of the Institute of Asia-Pacific Studies, Chinese Academy of Social Sciences (CASS), China. His research area is in institutional economics and international political economy. He gained his PhD in economics from the Graduate School of CASS in 1991. He has published widely in the areas of institutional economics, international political economy, and China's economic security.

Introduction

Masahisa Fujita

In the march of globalization in the world economy, the regional economic integrations which have been progressing institutionally in the EU and the Americas are now substantially under way among countries in Asia, including Japan, Korea, China and the ASEAN countries too. India, often compared to a Gigantic Elephant, has also taken steps on its passage towards economic integration. By substantially raising its trade and investments in the Asian markets, this Elephant may walk faster than ever and come to play an important role in the progress of Asia's economic integration. India's full-scale participation in the Asian market will affect other East Asian countries, which in turn will also have manifold influences on India.

India initiated economic reforms in 1991 and gave up the import substitution strategy which she had followed since independence. This was the turning point from which India started to adjust her economy to globalization; previously the Indian market had been distorted by regulations and was dormant. The purpose of the economic reforms was to activate the market through competition, and india tried to introduce advanced technology from developed countries through foreign direct investment and increase her exports.

After the industrial licensing regulation, which had limited investment in the manufacturing sector, had been swept away, there was a boom in investment in the manufacturing sector, particularly in consumer durable goods industries. The investment promoted growth of production, and the manufacturing sector maintained growth rates of gross value-added around 10 per cent. However, after reaching a peak in 1996, investment declined.

In sharp contrast with the manufacturing sector, investment in the service sector has risen since the end of the 1990s and the sector has grown rapidly. Primary, secondary and tertiary industries accounted for 34 per cent, 24 per cent and 42 per cent of GDP respectively in 1991; and 21 per cent, 27 per cent, and 52 per cent respectively in 2004, during which period the principal industry shifted from agriculture to service. On the other hand, industrial structure of the workforce presents a different picture. The primary, secondary and tertiary industries accounted for 62 per cent, 15 per cent, and 23 per cent respectively of the total labour force in 1999, which means that agriculture account for a large proportion of the underemployed workforce, which cannot get sufficient income to survive. Agriculture is still very important in India.

India has actively approached ASEAN in the twenty-first century; for example the Indo-ASEAN summit has been held back-to-back with the annual ASEAN Summit since 2002, and the first East Asia Summit took place in December 2005. The Government of India will maintain its 'Look East Policy'. One reason why India is approaching ASEAN is to attract foreign direct investment from developed countries. The domestic market is not large in spite of a population of one billion, and the investment boom of the mid-1990s was over after utilization of capacity decreased and over-investment emerged. Domestic demand did not increase as much as expected. Exports therefore become important as an outlet, but India does not have neighbouring countries with big domestic markets. If India's economic integration with ASEAN progresses, foreign direct investment may flow into India to capture not only the domestic market but also the ASEAN market.

At the same time, economic integration might have a reverse effect. As economic integration makes exporting from ASEAN to India easier, some foreign companies may withdraw from India. In fact, a Japanese company closed down its unit in India and its units in Thailand started to export to India. Indian companies must improve international competitiveness *vis-à-vis* foreign companies to grow further under globalization. The industrial world is keen to take advantage of the business opportunities created by economic integration with North-East Asia and ASEAN. Although the Indian media argued against the inflow of Chinese goods around 2000, calling it a threat, our main contention is that foreign trade with China is an expansion of business opportunities.

The Institute of Developing Economies (IDE-JETRO), Asahi Shimbun and the World Bank organized an international symposium entitled 'Economic Integration in Asia and India' in Tokyo on 8 December 2005. This symposium specifically focused on how Asian countries would be affected by India's participation in economic integration, how India itself would be affected domestically in this process, and, finally, explored the ways in which the region could successfully pave the way towards economic integration. This book has grown out of the proceedings of the symposium.

Jagdish Bhagwati points out that the East Asian economy has developed taking advantage of foreign trade, but unless multilateralism is guaranteed it cannot maintain its growth on the basis of foreign trade. He expects East Asian countries to assert that non-trade issues such as labour standards, environment rules and capital flow control should be discussed at the Doha Round of the WTO. Homi Kharas argues that as high productivity sectors are different in East Asia, East Asian countries compensate for their weak sectors by economic cooperation. Zhang Yuyan contends that although foreign trade between China and India is beneficial for both countries, domestic interest groups are obstacles to the development of foreign trade between them. Chularat Suteethorn points out the possibility of economic cooperation between Thailand and India, while Shuji Uchikawa finds that, though India is benefiting from globalization, poverty in some unirrigated areas creates trade conflict on palm oil imports from Malaysia and Indonesia. Ramesh Chand discusses the bottleneck of agricultural growth in India.

In the dynamic economic integration process under way in East Asia, there are various interesting aspects worthy of study. We hope that this book touches on some of them and will be happy if it contributes to further understanding some of the issues involved.

1

India, Japan and Asia

Jagdish Bhagwati

When I had to write a Preface for the Japanese edition of one of my books, I wrote that there were three countries for which I had an attachment: India where I come from, the United States which I now live in, and Japan.

I became interested in Japan when I was appointed Secretary, in 1962, to the Indian Wise Men Committee on Indo-Japanese Collaboration and went to Japan for a month where I interacted with Saburo Okita, a distinguished and cosmopolitan bureaucrat, who was my counterpart as Secretary to the Japanese Wise-Men Committee. I was taken to Kyoto, Nara, Osaka and other cities, slept on *tatamis* at Japanese Inns, saw Noh and Kabuki plays, and began reading Japanese literature, seeing Japanese films and studying Japanese transition to economic prowess.

When Japan-bashing began in the United States in the 1980s, my bonding with Japan, and my knowledge of Japanese culture and economics intensified yet further. By then I had joined the Economics Department at MIT as a Professor of Economics in 1968, where I became the principal defender of Japan against the indiscriminate attacks on her as an 'unfair trader', excluding imports and dumping exports.

But I offer this contribution, not as a scholar of US–Japan economic interaction, but rather in a reversion to the earlier phase of my life as a long-standing scholar of the economies of India and Japan, putting the current situation and the future prospects of the interaction between the two great countries in the wider context of Asia.

India's growth: past, present and future

Let me first begin with India's growth performance. Why emphasize growth? As many of you may be aware, my view has been that, given India's considerable poverty, growth is essential to reduce poverty. Whereas the left-radicals contemptuously refer to growth as a passive, conservative 'trickle-down' strategy, suggesting that we are all enjoying a banquet and a few crumbs fall into the hands and mouths of the impoverished serfs huddled below the table, I have always argued (since the early 1960s when I was working on the problem of poverty reduction in the Indian Planning Commission) that growth is a radical and activist 'pull-up' strategy where considerable state effort is put into accelerating the growth rate so that poverty can be impacted.

Growth reduces poverty directly, by creating jobs which the poor can access; it also reduces it indirectly because it adds to the budgetary revenues that can then be spent on health, education and other social spending which can improve the living standards of the poor. As the current Indian Prime Minister Manmohan Singh has also emphasized, it is all very well to ask for more social spending for the poor but, without growth, that demand can be made but it is almost impossible to respond to.

The problem in India was not with its growth-to-reduce-poverty strategy. The problem was with the fact that the economic policies pursued did not produce the growth in the first place! India, for a variety of reasons which I have explored in my book, *India in Transition* (Clarendon Press: Oxford, 1993, chapter 1), adopted a policy framework that *undermined* growth. These policies mainly included:

- a shift to autarky so that India's share of world exports fell, as did the share of trade in her national income, when many other nations improved their export performance;
- a Kafkaesque expansion of import, production and investment controls *via* a restrictive licensing system known then as 'permit *Raj*', so that competition and innovation were stifled;
- an enormous expansion of the public sector into areas well-beyond utilities and 'natural monopolies', into several industries, with huge losses that added to macroeconomic fiscal imbalances and to industrial efficiency also, because many of the public-sector enterprises produced intermediates (such as steel) which entered other industries and affected their operations adversely in turn; and

- a jaundiced view of inward flow of direct equity investment, and attendant restrictions on it, so much so that when the 1991 shift to reforms began, the annual equity investment inflow was less than $100 million, believe it or not![1]

The result during almost a quarter of a century was an economic *debacle* (while the Far Eastern economies, which had diametrically different policies, registered an economic *miracle*) of abysmal growth rates, fluctuating around an average of 3.5 per cent annually. Given the population growth rate around 2 per cent that left an increase of per capita income of 1.5 per cent annually. It takes only commonsense, not economic sophistication, to see that in such a stagnant economy, poverty will not diminish either; and it did not. Ironically, Indian economists such as Professor Amartya Sen persisted in defending, implicitly or explicitly, these outrageously counterproductive policies, catering to pseudo-left forces, and wound up increasing Indian poverty and then presenting themselves to the ignorant public as the champions of the poor whose numbers they had themselves multiplied!

Starting with some reforms in the 1980s, but principally with the acceleration of these reforms initiated in 1991, the Indian economy has moved into higher gears, raising the average growth rate to almost 6–6.5 per cent. With this, poverty has declined, both in rural and in urban sectors. The only debate in India now is on how much poverty has declined, not *regarding* whether it has.

But if India is no longer a basket case and nearly twenty years of high growth, as also the astonishing success of its IT industry, have turned the country's image around, one cannot extrapolate this into a forecast of continuing acceleration of India's performance. Four comments, all rather sobering about India's prospects, are in order.

First, while India has removed licensing and has reduced its trade barriers from an average of nearly 75 per cent applied tariff on manufactured goods down to nearly 15 per cent today, its ability to remove the restrictions on foreign equity investment has been handicapped by continuing bureaucratic hassles. At the same time, India has become stuck with its public sector enterprises as efforts at privatization have been checkmated by the right-wing forces in the BJP (the Bharatiya Janata Party), which lost the last elections but was in power till then and the left-wing coalition partners of the Congress Party (which won the last election but has a coalition with the Communist parties). The

Congress Party is also unable to move forward on much-needed labour reforms which make even the absurdly inefficient French and German labour market practices look good by contrast! This illustrates the point that, while democracies can do well on development,[2] they are unable to change course with ease (whereas dictatorships like in China can, relatively speaking, as witnessed by China's more drastic reforms under Deng) because the old mix of institutions and 'interests' (i.e. vested interests or lobbies), that have grown up around the 'old model' which one is trying to discard, proposes and poses serious political difficulties in making the transition to a 'new model'.

Third, the infrastructure problems which India faces are quite enormous. It is still an open question whether, given the general prevalence of near-xenophobic views about foreign investment, India can make a substantial inroad into this bottleneck to raising its growth rate still further beyond 6.5 per cent annually on a sustained basis. Note that China does not face this problem.

Finally, the opposition to further reform comes from within the Congress Party itself. 1991 saw a displacement of socialist sentiments and of the proponents of the mix of policies. But now, on the false assumption (as I will presently argue) that it was the BJP reforms – which in fact were simply carrying forward those initiated in 1991 by the Congress Party itself – that drove the BJP defeat, the discarded socialists of the Congress Party have now flocked around the powerful Congress leader, Sonia Gandhi. This has a parallel to the Bush 43 administration bringing into its fold the dissatisfied conservative hawks from the Bush 41 administration: Cheney *et al.* These socialist hawks are allying themselves with the coalition partners outside the Congress Party, the Communists, to stall further reforms. Why are they powerful enough to stall further reforms?

They have come back from the cold because the assumption which the Congress leadership around Sonia Gandhi has bought into is that it was the 'neoliberal' reforms that led to a neglect of the poor in the rural areas and therefore we need to reject the emphasis on these reforms and do rural development. I do not buy into this thesis at all. Nearly all incumbent governments at the State level, whether BJP or Congress, lost. In short, the incumbents were being thrown out, whether they had been introducing modern reforms or not. My hypothesis, which I advanced (with Professor Panagariya) in an article in the *Wall Street Journal* within days of the election results, in response to anti-reforms claims of novelists such as Salman Rushdie and Arundhati Roy, who in my view were continuing to write fiction when commenting on election results, was that the results reflected instead the success of the reforms in reducing poverty. As long as the economy grew poorly before the reforms were introduced, poverty was barely reduced. So, there was what I called a 'non-revolution of falling expectations': the poor felt dispirited and said to themselves: that is the way it is. But once the reforms began to deliver results, we had the 'revolution of perceived possibilities', or the 'revolution of rising expectations': the poor saw that they could improve their lot and now wanted more. Oliver Twist also wanted more but had to settle for less. But the poor with votes could ask for more and turn out the incumbents as they asked for more.

There is nothing wrong with shifting the state's attention to the rural sector. But if this is done, as the people around Sonia Gandhi are doing, by floating expensive 'employment guarantee schemes' which are soaking up huge sums of money, many susceptible to stereotypical diversion into corruption – more so than in the case of output-enhancing infrastructure projects where at least there is visible output to check against, whereas employment enhancing schemes can be judged only by expenditure and apparent employment – then there is likely to be a considerable damage done by diversion of funds from more productive rural uses. The tendency of the Indian political scene to revert back to pseudo-socialist chatter and policies that can harm the economy is disturbing; and only time will determine whether the sensible pro-reform views of the Prime Minister and his allies such as the Finance Minister or the revived anti-reform proclivities of the erstwhile defunct socialists will prevail.

India and China

The question arises, and is relevant to what I discuss later below, as to whether India will ever catch up with China. Both were sleeping giants who were expected at the beginning of the postwar period to awaken and become great players. As it happened, they both fell into counterproductive policies, among them a shared refusal to take advantage of the opportunities offered by globalization. China did this for political reasons – communist regimes such as the Soviet Union and Maoist China turned away from integrating themselves into the world economy, the way North Korea has done for decades. On the other hand, India did so because of bad choices in economic policy (as discussed above). In the meantime, it was the Far Eastern Four instead who, by shifting to outward orientation from the late 1950s, turned into the new and lean giants; turning into economic miracles indeed.

Finally, almost four decades late, India and China have woken up. But except for Thomas Friedman, few expect India to get close in performance to China soon: it is China that sends shock waves everywhere. Consider Lee Kuan Yew's remarks in New Delhi this summer:

> In the decade from 1994 to 2004, India's GDP grew two-fold from US$ 310 billion to US$ 661 billion. But during the same period, China's GDP grew three-fold from US$ 542 billion to US$ 1,649 billion. In 1984, India's GDP was about 30% smaller than China's. A decade later, it was more than 40% smaller and by 2004 it was about 60% smaller.

But what is the prognosis for the medium and long run? China does not have the rule of law; India has. The authoritarian structure of China carries its own costs. I recall my wife, Professor Padma Desai, talking on a Panel on India and China when both Mao and Chou En Lai were alive. Asked what would be China's trajectory on economic and political development, she said: it depends on whether Mao or Chou En Lai dies first. The Chinese system is top heavy, non-transparent and hence fragile and volatile; India's is at an advantage on these fronts.

Then again, will China really be able to hack it in an IT-intensive world when it is constantly worried about how information technology in the hands of its people may be subversive? India is a democracy and her IT sector has worked wonders. But China has fallen behind. The reason is that the PC and the CP (the Communist Party) are basically incompatible. Again, authoritarian structures can become very expensive except in cases where basically sound decisions are taken, as in China with her reforms during the 1980s. But all is not rosy there either. China's savings rate is estimated today as close to 50 per cent: a number which seems absurdly large and hence unreliable. But that the number is larger than India's 25 per cent or thereabouts. But China's growth rate is not commensurately large. So, presumably India uses resources-cum-investments more efficiently than China.

Finally, as China's middle class grows dramatically, it is likely to become restless for political liberty, in a classic fashion. How will the political dictatorship react to it? Will it try to repress these demands, leading to Falun Gong type of problems and disruption of the state? Or will the process be smooth and evolutionary, with the Communist Party accommodating gradually to the political demands for more democracy? We cannot know; but there is as much likelihood of China's miracle collapsing as of its continuing.

All this makes many observers today feel that India, while now behind China on the escalator, should get ahead in the longer run. But that the two powers are here to stay, and to become with Japan the three major giants in the Asian region is a moral certainty. What does this imply?

India, China and Japan: major Asian powers

Clearly, the postwar expectation that Japan would be the most important player in Asia, with Asia and especially ASEAN countries as part of its 'co-prosperity' sphere (of influence and responsibility), has to be modified to include India and China in the equation. Asia now is getting its **Big Three**.

From an ASEAN perspective, this is all to the good. Only one hegemon in your front yard is always anxiety-creating. An oligopoly of hegemons helps: each competes with the others for influence, replacing the itch to dominate and intimidate with the itch to please and seduce. The biggest hegemon of all, the United States, which is concerned about the rise of China for many reasons, would like to use Japan and the new India to act as a counterweight to China, to see these two enormous Asian tigers, one old and the other new, 'contain' China. Evidently neither India nor Japan wants to play, nor be seen as playing, that kind of role. Both countries have to live with China; it is surely not in their national interest to get into an adversarial position *vis-à-vis* China.

India and Japan: 'natural allies'

But India and Japan will surely act, without much fuss, as such counterweights to China. After all, the two nations have been Asia's most important democracies since the end of the Second World War. Among the developing countries, India is unique: where nearly all newly independent and other developing countries at some stage abandoned democracy, India remained wedded to it. Now that many of these countries have come to be democracies one might also think that India's democracy would be less valued. But it is more so, for India is regarded as having been the precursor of this new trend. And her ability to function as a democracy despite her many religions, languages and ethnicities is regarded as a triumph. By contrast, China's authoritarianism seems like an anachronism; and her human-rights abuses as much as her lack of democracy reduce her appeal.

Their democracies make India and Japan 'natural allies'. So does their ambition now to get permanent Security Council seats: they plus Germany and Brazil have joined hands in this quest. The fact that China is lukewarm, at best, in her support for this move is yet another reason why India and Japan get closer politically.

But, aside from the political factors, there also are economic reasons for a growing closeness between India and Japan. As China has become more unruly in her Japan-bashing, claiming that Japan does not repent enough for her Second World War atrocities and protesting against Japan with riots, it is clear that Japan would have a legitimate interest in diversifying away from excessive dependence on China as a location for her corporations.

Evidently, India offers a better destination for such overseas manufacture by Japanese firms. Unlike China, and indeed much of Asia, India has no unpleasant memories of the Japanese during the Second World War: there is no such memory because there is almost nothing to remember! The Japanese eastward march got bogged down in the jungles of Burma for the most part; and except for the north-eastern border India was not a witness to Japanese invasion. So there is no resentment such as in China where the memory of the war is intolerable and Japan is barely tolerated. India therefore is not merely a 'naturally' but also a 'natural' location for Japanese firms in seeking labour-abundant locations for parts of their manufacture.

Indeed, this should have happened on a larger scale, much earlier. But the fault lay in India's dirigiste state, with masses of restrictions. Today, however, growing reforms have changed that situation. Not enough, as I said earlier, on the foreign-investment front. But the left-wing opposition to such investment can be more readily surmounted for Japanese firms, in bilateral initiatives, than for Western firms which come from 'imperialist' countries. As it happens, the Prime Minister Manmohan Singh succeeded me as the Secretary to the Indian Wise

Men's Committee. The time has come for a major breakthrough of economic relations between the two countries.

Bilateral trade agreements in Asia: India, China and Japan

How does the prospect look then for Asian trade liberalization, as part of Asian economic integration? And what is India's and Japan's role in it? A few points can be made:

1 *Why Preferential Trade Agreements (PTAs) are bad news*: Asia long held out against bilateral free trade agreements which are now called what they really are: Preferential Trade Agreements. But it has now joined in the '*Great PTA Rush*'. Why are these PTAs a curse? Let me explain.

First, note that PTAs liberalize trade for the member countries and therefore that part is a freeing of trade. But they also increase, for any given external tariffs, the handicap suffered by non-members in the members' markets. These then are tantamount to increasing protection against non-members. So, PTAs are two-faced: they free trade for members and they increase protection against non-members. So, as Jacob Viner (1950) pointed out in a seminal contribution in the 1950s, PTAs are different from non-discriminatory, non-preferential freeing of trade.

They therefore can divert trade from efficient non-members with low costs of production and can harm those joining such a union (by increasing the cost of their imports), non-members (whose exports are diverted) and world efficiency (by shifting production from lower-cost non-members to higher-cost members). There is plenty of evidence of such trade diversion from specific PTAs.

Second, and far more important, when PTAs multiply, there is a 'systemic' problem: they badly bust up the multilateral system represented by MFN treatment for all members of the GATT, now the WTO. When you have nearly 300 such PTAs today, and they are increasing by the week, most-favoured-nation (MFN) tariffs become terribly emasculated: they matter less and less. Tariffs depend on where a product comes from: for example a country has 12 PTAs and therefore, for any product, there are likely to be 12 different tariff rates at any point of time, depending on the trajectory of each PTA. Then again, if a different tariff applies to a product from a particular preferred source, then the product must be determined to have originated from that source: so we have rules of origin. So, we also have countless and occasionally sector-wise-differentiated rules of origin that are basically arbitrary. So, between different tariff rates and different rules of origin, you have chaos in the tariff structure. This is what I have called the 'spaghetti bowl' problem.

The MFN principle, so central to the trading system we built after the War, has now been decimated.

Third, the hegemonic powers, the EU and the USA, have used the PTAs with small countries to establish templates on non-trade issues such as labour standards, environmental rules, capital flow controls and so on which are not in the WTO, while also demanding WTO+ (i.e. WTO plus) obligations on issues such as intellectual property protection where the issues are in the WTO already. The trade game is converted, through tough negotiations with small countries, by dangling preferential market access before them, into a non-trade game. It is notable that the PTAs among the developing countries by themselves typically do not have such non-trade issues included in their agreements. The big developing countries such as Brazil and India have rejected these nefarious tactics and the intended intrusion of these non-trade issues so far at the WTO. It is notable also that the PTAs planned by Japan and China do not, to my knowledge, include these extraneous, non-trade issues.

2 *Asian PTAs*: The EU started doing PTAs; then the USA, instead of objecting to them – it had the necessary power to do so at the GATT – joined in with enthusiasm, the main culprits being Secretary Jim Baker and his Deputy Robert Zoellick. As US Trade Representative, Zoellick did his best to proliferate them further, claiming mistakenly that PTAs were good for the multilateral trading system as they would prod the world into multilateral trade negotiations.

And now, quite predictably, Asia has joined the process, with China and Japan taking major initiatives with them and India also beginning to consider them actively. For Japan this is a major departure, as it is for the ASEAN countries of APEC, because at the APEC they had all agreed on maintaining MFN and concerted MFN liberalization rather than turning the APEC countries into a Preferential Trading Bloc under Article 24 of the GATT. This is partly a matter of 'monkey see, monkey do'; but it is also an instance of 'reactive PTA formation', where Asia excludes market access from its groupings the way the US PTAs, and the proposed Free Trade Area of the Americas will exclude Asia and others. The fault lies with the USA and its mindless and intellectually defective leadership, not with Japan, China and now India.

3 *Importance of Doha Round and multilateral reduction of trade barriers*: The proliferation of PTAs in the Asian region is not an ideal way to liberalize trade, for the many reasons I have stated above. In particular, China, which is technically a developing country, needs to remember that it needs nonetheless to subject its own PTAs with other developing countries to the discipline of Article 24, instead of using the much weaker and self-destructive route offered by the Enabling Clause to PTAs exclusively among the developing countries.

But the surest way to eliminate some of the deleterious trade consequences of PTA proliferation is to push hard to make the Doha Round a success. As the poorest countries who enjoy preferences now finally understand, MFN trade liberalization reduces the effectiveness of preferences; the preferences are relative to the MFN tariff so that a zero MFN tariff means zero *de facto* preference. So, the only effective way of killing preferences is to kill the MFN tariff: a ratio can be affected by working on the numerator or the denominator. So, the ultimate contribution that Asia can make to undo the damage that Zoellick and the Europeans have wreaked on the world trading system through bilateral PTAs is to provide the leadership to reduce MFN tariffs further by making the Doha Round a success.

Notes

1 The diagnosis of these policies, and their adverse implications for Indian economic performance, was made in *India: Planning for Industrialization* (Oxford University Press, 1968) that Professor Padma Desai and I wrote several years before the reforms started in India.

2 See the extended analysis I have offered in my Rajiv Gandhi Golden Jubilee Memorial Lecture, 22 October 1994 in New Delhi, titled 'Democracy and Development: New Thinking on an Old Question', reprinted as chapter 40 in my collected essays, *A Stream of Windows* (Cambridge, Mass., MIT Press, 1998). Senior Minister Lee Kuan Yew of Singapore, the architect of Singapore's miracle, also addresses this question with insight in a splendid Nehru Memorial Lecture that he gave this year in New Delhi.

Reference

Viner, Jacob (1950) *The Customs Union Issue*. New York: Carnegie Endowment for International Peace.

2
East Asia: Regional Integration among Open Economies

*Homi Kharas, Enrique Aldaz-Carroll and Sjamsu Rahardja**

Introduction

East Asian economies have made the notion of 'export-led growth' almost synonymous with 'development' over the past forty years. Export-led growth, in turn, has become an indication of growing economic integration with the rest of the world, and has led to the present situation where the emerging economies of East Asia have one of the highest export/GDP ratios of any grouping of countries in the world, at 41 per cent, and where East Asia, including Japan, now accounts for one-quarter of the world's exports. Given this success, economic integration seems to be a well-established phenomenon in the region.

Yet this chapter will argue that East Asia's integration is changing perceptibly. Economic integration within the region is growing much more strongly, and at the same time regionalism, or formal economic cooperation among countries in the region, is growing. These developments raise questions about how economic integration should be assessed. While most economists are strong believers that significant welfare gains are associated with general economic integration with the rest of the world ('openness'), there is no such presumption that regional economic

* The authors (hkharas@worldbank.org, ealdazcarroll@worldbank.org, srahardja@worldbank.org) would like to thank Swati Ghosh and Arvind Gupta for helpful comments. Thanks are also due to Walter Meza-Cuadra, Radu Tatucu, Santiago Gomez and Antonio Ollero for their research assistance. The findings, interpretations and conclusions in this chapter are those of the authors; they do not necessarily represent the views of the World Bank, its Executive Directors, or the countries that they represent and should not be attributed to them.

integration brings with it similar welfare benefits. That depends on the nature of regional integration and is the topic of this chapter.

We argue below that closer regional integration within East Asia is being driven principally by market forces. We postulate that a rapid fall in transport costs and other barriers to international trade are creating new regional production networks that are consistent with greater efficiency in production and hence with so-called dynamic gains from trade. There appears to be considerable scope for this process to extend further into new sectors and new countries, with China playing an increasingly important role.

Measuring integration is always complicated. We start from the assumption that a high level of integration is found when economies have three characteristics – a high degree of trade in goods, co-movement of the price of capital and similarity of services regimes. These characteristics ensure allocative efficiency and support high volumes of trade in goods, capital and services. In the next section we look at intraregional trade, and use gravity models to assess whether East Asia trades more within the region than expected, given the size and openness of these economies and their geographic proximity to each other. We find that not only is the East Asia dummy variable significant, but that it may be increasing over time, a finding that is attributed to the growth in trade in parts and components which we separately analyse. We then turn to foreign direct investment and show that the integration of trade in goods is associated with a growing stock of intra-regional FDI. China is the main recipient of FDI in East Asia and most of China's inflows come from other East Asian countries. China and the newly industrializing economies (NIEs) are also emerging as a major FDI source for other countries in the region, and this is likely to intensify.

We then turn to the second measure of integration, and look at whether prices, in this instance for equities, move together across the region. We base this discussion on a 'news' study of regional equity markets. We find that the impact of regional news has increased since the 1997 financial crisis. This is taken as further corroboration that the real economies in the region are seen by investors as having integrated outlooks.

We then move on to consider trade in services. Here, we use the third measure of integration, namely the similarity in the policy and regulatory regimes. East Asia is a region where there exist considerable implicit and explicit regulatory practices favouring domestic service providers. Services liberalization has lagged behind goods liberalization and productivity in services tends to be low. We show that India has a significant comparative advantage in services trade, which offers the prospect of a mutually beneficial trade between East Asian exporters of merchandise goods and Indian exporters of services. As is the case for parts and components, services imports offers the potential for productivity gains as well as allocative efficiency gains from trade, multiplying the welfare gains.

A final section concludes. In common with many other observers, the evidence in this chapter leads us to conclude that East Asian economic integration will continue to yield efficiency gains for goods and financial systems. Substantial additional benefits could accrue if countries were to aggressively pursue services liberalization, in which case it is more attractive for India to become more closely integrated with East Asia.

Trade in goods integration

Evolution of East Asia's extraregional and intraregional trade

An important driving force behind Emerging East Asia's[1] successful growth has long been rapid and sustained growth in international trade (World Bank, 1993, 2003). This trend was maintained over 1994–2004, a period characterized by higher than world average growth rates in both exports and GDP, despite the dramatic losses in many countries associated with the 1997 financial crisis. As a result, East Asian economies' share of world exports grew 1.8 percentage points over the period.

It is important to note that we treat China and Hong Kong as one country denoted 'China & Hong Kong'. Since Hong Kong plays an important role as a trade relay centre for mainland China, treating both economies separately would bias our results towards finding an expansion in intra-regional trade, since it is well-known that more than 80 per cent of exports from Hong Kong are re-exports, and that re-exports originating in China account for more than 50 per cent of all exports (Isogai and Shibanuma, 2004).

Table 2.1 shows three salient characteristics of economic performance over the last decade. First, there has been rapid GDP growth (in current US dollar terms) in emerging East Asia (4.8% p.a.), but this is concentrated in Hong Kong and Vietnam. Korea, Taiwan, China and the rest of Southeast Asia grew more slowly than the world average. Second, growth in trade tells a very different story. Most of

Table 2.1 Growth rates and shares of exports, imports and GDP

	Average annual growth rate 1994–2004 (%)					*Export to GDP ratio (%)*		*Imports to GDP ratio (%)*		*Share in world exports (%)*		*Share in world imports (%)*	
	Exports	*Imports*	*Exports to emerging East Asia*	*Imports from emerging East Asia*	*GDP*	*1994–96*	*2002–04*	*1994–96*	*2002–04*	*1994–96*	*2002–04*	*1994–96*	*2002–04*
World*	5.86	6.24	6.22	7.34	3.17	16.68	20.38	16.97	21.29	100.00	100.00	100.00	100.00
EU	5.84	6.17	3.14	8.31	2.35	27.75	36.38	26.76	35.81	41.58	41.79	39.42	39.32
South Asia	8.76	9.37	9.27	9.76	5.41	9.62	12.29	11.83	15.76	0.93	1.15	1.12	1.41
India	10.08	11.80	11.27	13.60	6.73	8.16	10.33	8.99	12.78	0.60	0.83	0.65	0.98
Japan	2.04	3.05	3.10	5.67	−1.25	8.47	11.25	6.51	9.08	8.75	6.49	6.56	5.01
USA	3.48	7.59	1.97	6.67	5.16	7.76	6.75	10.29	12.17	11.98	10.03	15.63	17.27
Emerging East Asia*	7.34	6.22	9.77	8.13	4.84	33.88	40.86	35.84	39.38	15.73	17.56	16.36	16.18
Cambodia	26.60	9.75	0.39	10.80	3.88	9.31	50.42	45.30	70.74	0.01	0.03	0.03	0.04
China & HK	10.89	10.93	13.53	10.64	8.67	26.55	31.18	28.74	33.57	4.56	6.68	4.86	6.88
Indonesia	4.49	−0.32	9.12	8.22	1.98	22.35	27.30	19.02	15.78	0.94	0.85	0.79	0.47
Korea Rep.	6.51	5.20	10.79	11.42	2.96	24.66	32.82	25.74	30.09	2.57	2.68	2.64	2.36
Lao PDR.	5.84	5.37	1.01	5.28	2.88	18.07	21.53	35.58	40.79	0.01	0.01	0.01	0.01
Malaysia	5.89	3.04	7.35	5.23	2.49	79.81	102.24	81.71	83.95	1.46	1.45	1.47	1.14
Philippines	10.23	4.29	22.72	8.93	1.30	23.06	45.81	37.22	48.13	0.36	0.50	0.56	0.50
Singapore	3.74	1.91	5.35	3.19	2.02	137.91	155.24	145.33	141.03	2.37	1.99	2.45	1.73
Taiwan, China	4.43	4.26	9.05	9.22	1.39	40.67	51.22	36.99	46.48	2.24	2.00	2.00	1.73
Thailand	5.87	2.66	9.24	4.94	−1.4	32.1	56.69	40.63	54.13	1.10	1.10	1.37	1.00
Vietnam	17.92	15.40	16.12	11.48	8.76	27.42	52.04	40.62	64.78	0.12	0.28	0.17	0.33

Note: *Trade between China and Hong Kong not computed. Data is in current US$. Growth rates are least-squares growth rates. Emerging East Asia grouping is integrated by all the East Asian countries presented below the group category. Data for exports to emerging East Asia and imports from emerging East Asia are mirror data reported by emerging East Asian countries.
Sources: Trade data from IMF, *Direction of Trade Statistics*; GDP data from *World Bank Global Development Finance* (GDF)/*World Development Indicators* (WDI).

emerging East Asia had more rapid growth of exports than the world average. Consequently, the export/GDP ratio in emerging East Asia (one measure of 'openness') has grown substantially to around 41 per cent, a level which places it above most other areas in the world including the EU. Each of the economies in the emerging East Asia group has increased their export/GDP ratios, in some cases, dramatically.

The third salient point is that exports of East Asian countries to emerging East Asia, and their imports from East Asia, have been growing much faster than their average export or import growth rates. The Philippines, Indonesia, Korea, and Taiwan, China have had intra-regional trade growing almost twice as fast as average trade over the last decade. Intra-regional exports, including Japan, are at 45 per cent, while intra-regional imports have risen even more rapidly. Emerging East Asia now sources more of its imports from within the region (52%) than is the case in NAFTA (37%) (Table 2.2).[2] China has been particularly

Table 2.2 Destination of exports and sources of imports (%)

	EA exports to		*EA imports from*	
	1994–96	*2002–04*	*1994–96*	*2002–04*
Intra-region	**44.11**	**45.25**	**46.93**	**52.48**
Cambodia	0.10	0.14	0.02	0.02
China & Hong Kong	10.10	13.85	6.03	9.79
Indonesia	1.51	1.31	2.28	2.34
Japan	9.21	8.83	17.05	14.36
Korea	4.23	4.65	4.78	6.25
Lao PD Rep.	0.04	0.04	0.02	0.01
Malaysia	4.09	3.34	4.03	4.36
Philippines	1.44	1.56	0.72	1.81
Singapore	5.67	4.01	3.86	3.63
Taiwan, China	4.01	4.15	5.46	6.62
Thailand	3.10	2.38	2.36	2.73
Vietnam	0.62	1.00	0.31	0.55
Extra-region	**55.89**	**54.75**	**53.07**	**47.52**
EU	15.87	16.81	15.13	12.41
India	0.74	1.10	0.84	1.05
South Asia	1.56	1.87	1.12	1.22
US	24.35	22.23	17.76	12.25
Rest of world	13.37	12.72	18.23	20.59
World	100	100	100	100

Note: Trade between China and Hong Kong not computed in the calculations. Region is defined as East Asia (= emerging East Asia + Japan).
Source: IMF, *Direction of Trade Statistics*.

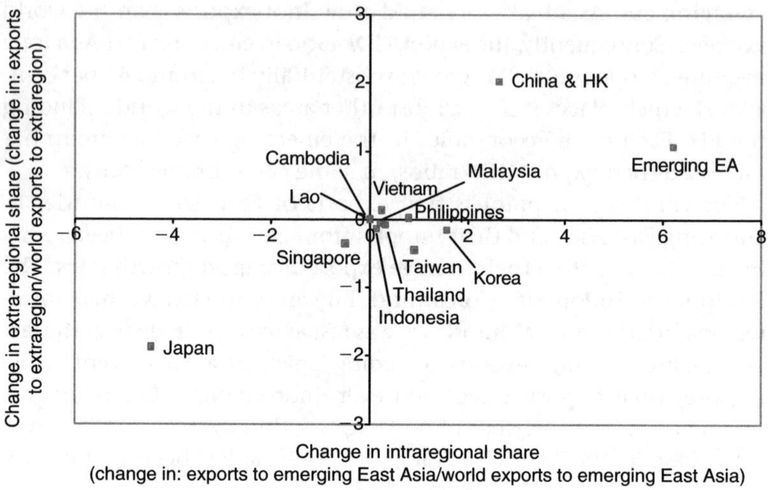

Figure 2.1 Percentage point change in intraregional and extraregional market shares between 1994–96 average and 2002–04 average (region = emerging East Asia)

dynamic – it is responsible for 42 per cent of the increase in intraregional imports. It is also significant that even though South Asia, and India in particular, have had very rapid growth in imports from East Asia, the share of East Asian exports going to South Asia remains very small. For emerging East Asian economies, the Philippines is still a bigger market for their goods exports than is India.

Emerging East Asia's growth of intraregional exports has not taken place at the expense of exports to the rest of the world, which have grown slightly above the world growth rate. As Figure 2.1 shows, East Asia has managed to increase both its world share in extraregional trade and its world share in intraregional trade, though the increase has been higher with respect to intraregional trade. This suggests that the region remains competitive *vis-à-vis* countries outside the region.

Explaining the growth of emerging East Asia's intraregional trade

Quantitatively, we can decompose emerging East Asia's intraregional export growth into changes in its export orientation, changes in its openness, and changes in its GDP. Thus, country *i*'s share in intraregional exports in year *t* can be expressed as:

$$X_{it}^{R} = \frac{X_{it}^{R}}{X_{it}^{W}} \frac{X_{it}^{W}}{GDP_{it}} GDP_{it} \tag{2-1}$$

Where X_{it}^{R} is country *i*'s nominal exports to the region at time *t*, X_{it}^{W} is country *i*'s nominal exports to the world at time *t*, and *GDP* is nominal GDP. Expressing equation (2-1) in logs and differentiating a country's export growth can be expressed as a function of the change in its export orientation, the change in its openness, and the change in its GDP:

$$\underset{\text{change in exports}}{d\log\left[X_i^R\right]} = \underset{\text{change in orientation}}{d\log\left[\frac{X_i^R}{X_i^W}\right]} + \underset{\text{change in openness}}{d\log\left[\frac{X_i^W}{GDP_i}\right]} + \underset{\text{change in economic size}}{d\log[GDP_i]} \tag{2-2}$$

This is simply an accounting identity. The decomposition shows that emerging East Asia's intraregional export growth is mostly due to the growth of emerging East Asian countries' GDP (which translates into a higher production supply and demand) and to a lesser extent to their greater opening to trade. The reorientation of exports towards the region has played a small, but important, part in the growth of intraregional exports (Table 2.3).

These broad calculations still do not tell us if there is something specific about East Asia that is driving increasing intraregional trade, or if the growth in intraregional trade is simply a reflection of the fact that these economies are among the world's most competitive exporters and are forming a 'natural bloc' (Frankel, Stein and Wei, 1997). To investigate this further, we try to explain East Asian trade through a regression analysis.

The regression specification employed is based on a gravity model. The basic gravity model postulates that trade between two economies grows proportionately with the size of the economies (captured by their GDP), with their per capita income levels, and, inversely, with the distance between them. A higher GDP is associated with a higher

Table 2.3 Decomposition of intraregional export growth, 1994–2004 (%)

	Growth of intraregional exports	*Intraregional export growth accounting for changes in*		
		Orientation	*Openness*	*GDP*
Emerging East Asia	102	11	28	64
Cambodia	19	−218	185	52
China & Hong Kong	133	12	22	99
Indonesia	73	15	20	38
Korea	124	33	44	47
Lao PDR	13	−45	14	45
Malaysia	85	8	31	46
Philippines	168	59	78	30
Singapore	72	10	20	41
Taiwan	98	36	40	22
Thailand	96	20	64	12
Vietnam	145	−40	83	102
Japan	56	20	39	−4

Note: Intraregion is defined as Emerging East Asia.
Source: Trade data from IMF, *Direction of Trade Statistics*; GDP data from *World Development Indicators*.

production capacity for export. A shorter distance is associated with lower transport and communication costs. Higher per capita income levels capture the fact that richer consumers desire greater variety in consumption leading to greater trade in differentiated products. Numerous empirical studies have used this specification and find these determinants of bilateral trade to be significant (for example Frankel and Wei, 1993; Rose, 2004). Frankel and Wei's (1993) study of bilateral trade flows among 63 countries for 1980, 1985, and 1990 also adds regional dummies and finds positive significant effects for the Western Hemisphere, the European Community, and East Asian dummies, indicating the presence of a regional bias in bilateral trade.

We follow this approach for each of the major East Asian markets. The specification employed is as follows:

$$\log(M_{ijt}) = \alpha + \beta_1 \log(GDP_{jt}) + \beta_2 \log(GDPCAP_{jt}) + \beta_3 \log(DIST_{ij}) + \beta_4 D_{EastAsia} + \varepsilon_{ijt} \quad (2\text{-}3)$$

where *i* denotes China & Hong Kong, Korea or Japan, *j* denotes any partner country in the world, *Mijt* denotes country *i*'s imports from country *j* at time *t*, GDP is the economic size of the partner country, GDPCAP is per capita GDP, DIST denotes distance between country *i* and *j* measured as the great-circle distance and DEast Asia is a dummy for East Asian partner countries.

The specification is run as a generalized least-squares regression. To allow for heteroscedasticity, the OLS standard errors are corrected using the Huber/White/Sandwich estimator of variance. Individual regressions are run for Japan, China & Hong Kong and Korea, which permits coefficients to differ across each of these markets. The regressions are run for 1994 and 2004 which allows us to also examine if the three countries' intraregional bias has changed over the period. Results are presented in Appendix 2. The distance data are taken from Rose (2004), GDP and GDPCAP are taken from the World Bank World Development Indicators and imports are taken from COMTRADE.

The regression results show all the key variables have their expected signs and significance. The sum of the coefficients on GDP and GDP per capita is typically greater than one, indicating that trade grows more than proportionately with economic growth. This captures to some extent the 'natural-bloc' effect previously mentioned. The impact of distance on bilateral trade has fallen between 1994 and 2004, which is consistent with the well-known fall in transport costs. As Figure 2.2 shows, transport costs, as measured by the difference between carriage, insurance, freight (CIF) and free on board (FOB) prices, have been falling steadily for years.

Table 2.4 shows the coefficients of the East Asia dummy variables for each of the three countries and for both years. In all cases, the coefficients are significantly different from zero, indicating that there is indeed a regional bias present. That is to say, imports from East Asia are higher than would be predicted by economic size, per capita income and distance alone. The diminishing effect of the regional bias in East Asia for 1980, 1985 and 1990 found by Frankel and Wei (1993) is not maintained between 1994 and 2004. The regional bias in 2004 is larger than in 1994 for China & Hong Kong and Japan, though this difference is not statistically significant.

One explanation for a regional bias is that trade increasingly reflects the emergence of regional production networks, in which parts and components are traded back and forth before final assembly. To

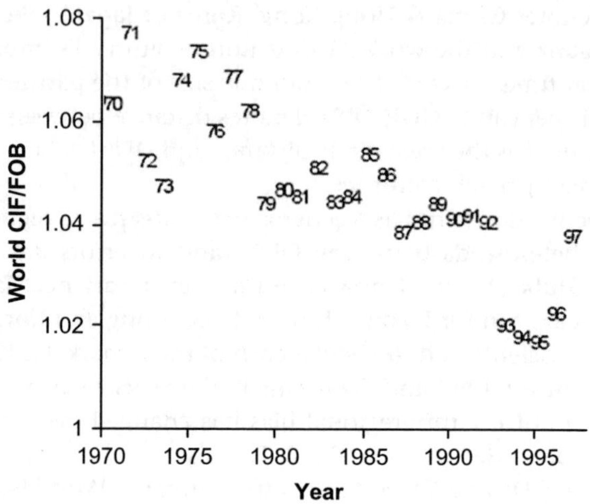

Figure 2.2 World transportation costs as measured by CIF/FOB ratios, 1970–98
Source: Hummels (1999).

investigate this, we follow Athukorala and Yamashita (2005) and separate the analysis between the imports of parts and components and imports of final goods (defined as total imports minus imports of parts and components). We then run for each country and year a regression for final goods and a regression for parts and components. The results indicate that China & Hong Kong, Korea and Japan all present an East Asian regional bias in their import of parts and components and that the coefficient is larger than for final goods, though the difference is not statistically significant (see Appendix 2). This indicates that trade in parts and components contributes to the regional bias in these countries' exports, but that it is not the only contributor to such bias, since the bias is also present in final goods exports. Our findings differ from those of Athukorala and Yamashita (2005). They run their regression for all East Asian countries simultaneously and employ one East Asian dummy for the whole region. They find that the East Asia dummy has a positive significant coefficient for parts and components, as in our regressions, but a negative and significant coefficient for final goods.

East Asia's parts and components trade is concentrated in a few economies. China has led the way, both as an importer (for final assembly) as well as an exporter. But the middle income East Asian

Table 2.4 Selected coefficients in generalized least-squares regressions

	China & Hong Kong				*Korea*				*Japan*			
	Total imports		*Imports parts & components*		*Total imports*		*Imports parts & components*		*Total imports*		*Imports parts & components*	
	(1)	(2)	(3)	(4)	(1)	(2)	(3)	(4)	(1)	(2)	(3)	(4)
Dependent variable	log imports 2004	log imports 1994	log imports 2004	log imports 1994	log imports 2004	log imports 1994	log imports 2004	log imports 1994	log imports 2004	log imports 1994	log imports 2004	log imports 1994
Dummy East Asia	2.27*** [0.59]	1.48*** [0.55]	2.96*** [0.95]	2.87*** [0.80]	2.44*** [0.63]	2.57*** [0.74]	2.83*** [0.65]	3.64*** [0.84]	2.66*** [0.56]	2.59*** [0.61]	3.38*** [0.94]	3.52*** [0.90]
Observations	123	120	62	62	131	131	66	66	141	141	79	79
Adjusted R-squared	0.75	0.76	0.82	0.80	0.73	0.64	0.78	0.77	0.73	0.74	0.76	0.73

Notes: Robust standard errors in brackets. * significant at 10%; ** significant at 5%; *** significant at 1%.

economies, Thailand, Philippines, Indonesia and Malaysia have also had rapid growth in their parts and components exports, as has Korea. This is a very different structure compared to the early 1990s when Japan, Hong Kong, Singapore and Taiwan, China accounted for 80 per cent of the region's parts and components exports.

Explaining China's changing role in the region

During the 1990s, China moved gradually to the production of labour-intensive goods through the assembly of parts and components. China & Hong Kong has experienced the highest growth in imports of parts and components in the region with an annual average growth rate of 19 per cent between 1994 and 2004 (Table 2.5). In

Table 2.5 Countries' share in East Asia's global trade in parts and components and growth rates of their exports and imports of parts and components

	Export share			*Import share*			*Average annual growth rates 1994–2004 (%)**	
	1994	*2001*	*2004*	*1994*	*2001*	*2004*	*Exports*	*Imports*
China & Hong Kong	26.3	40.4	53.7	29.5	40.5	47.5	16.76	13.56
China	4.9	13.4	23.1	12.1	20.1	27.2	28.49	17.87
Hong Kong	21.4	27.0	30.6	17.4	20.4	20.3	12.54	10.11
Indonesia	0.7	1.5	1.1	4.3	1.7	1.6	15.68	−5.21
Japan	45.6	30.0	26.5	13.8	15.7	13.5	1.17	7.85
Korea, Rep.	6.7	9.8	13.9	9.1	7.2	6.8	18.83	4.72
Malaysia	5.8	7.7	5.4	13.1	10.8	10.1	9.09	5.30
Philippines	0.7	2.5	1.4	2.8	6.2	6.8	17.49	15.89
Singapore	11.5	9.7	8.7	17.5	12.9	12.2	3.87	3.38
Taiwan, China	3.6	4.5	3.9	9.4	7.1	5.9	5.86	6.57
Thailand	10.4	10.4	8.2	5.9	5.7	5.4	8.97	2.08
East Asia	100	100	100	100	100	100	7.76	7.80

Note: East Asia refers here to the 9 countries in the table. Lao PDR, Cambodia and Vietnam have been excluded for lack of data. 2004 data for Thailand is based on mirror data. Exports are measured as gross exports (= exports + reexports). Trade between China and Hong Kong not computed.

* Least-squares average annual growth rates. Growth rates for Philippiness and Thailand are for the 1994 to 2003 period. East Asia aggregate for 2004 is estimated assuming the latter two countries grow at the same average growth rate as the other countries.

Source: United Nations Commodity Trade Statistics Database COMTRADE, SITC Rev. 2.

the early 1990s, the Chinese authorities indicated that the import of parts and components had a major strategic role in the country's overall trade policy (Ng and Yeats, 2003: 7):

> trade in components was encouraged by governmental policies, such as tariff exemptions, that viewed local assembly of foreign produced components as a means of entering markets for high skill or high technology products that would otherwise be impenetrable. Imports of components were also viewed as a means of improving the foreign competitiveness of other industries by lowering production costs.

In the mid-1980s and early 1990s, China and other emerging East Asian economies started applying more favourable FDI policies. Kawai (2005) notes that the contribution of FDI to export expansion in China and in middle-income ASEAN countries has been much larger than that experienced by the NIEs, which relied more heavily on R&D as a channel for technological upgrading. In 1990 the shares of foreign affiliates in total manufactured exports were approximately 20 per cent for the NIEs, while the corresponding shares for the middle-income ASEAN members and China were significantly higher, within the range of 30–90 per cent.

The role of foreign affiliates has been explored by Gaulier *et al.* (2005), who show that the share of foreign affiliates in China's exports has doubled over the last ten years, to reach 60 per cent today. A similar pattern is seen for imports. But foreign affiliates also report their processing trade, which comprises largely parts and components. There, too, the dramatic expansion in exports is clearly visible (Figure 2.3).

Gaulier *et al.* also report on the destination of exports from foreign affiliates and the sources of imports to these firms (Figure 2.4). The difference between Asia and the rest of the world is striking. Exports are going to the advanced economies in the EU and the USA (and Japan) while imports are being sourced from Asia. Kawai and Urata (2004) associate this with the nationality of the multinational corporation (MNC). Using 1997 data, they show that intrafirm trade is much more prevalent amongst Japanese MNCs than amongst EU or US firms, and that as much as 96 per cent of the total trade between Japanese affiliates and Japan are between the affiliate and the parent firm.

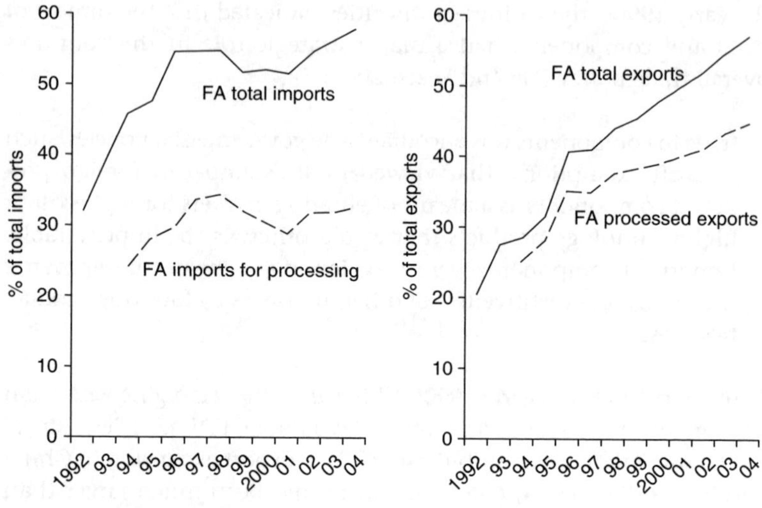

Figure 2.3 Share of foreign affiliates (FA) in total China's trade, 1992–2004
Source: Gaulier *et al.* (2005).

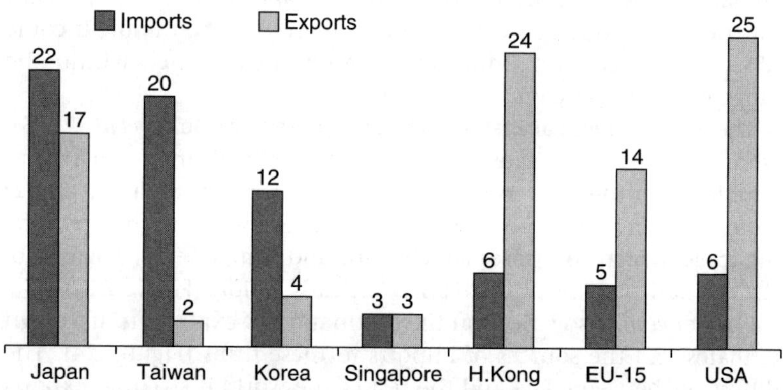

Figure 2.4 Processing trade of foreign affiliate firms in China by partner country, 2002 (% of processing imports or exports)
Note: The re-exportations of Hong Kong are not adjusted here.
Source: Gaulier *et al.* (2005).

The result of this FDI strategy has been a notable technological upgrading of China's exports. Table 2.6 classifies exports by industry of origin into four main categories with increasing skill, technology, capital and scale intensity (see Mayer, Butkevicius and Kadri, 2002,

Table 2.6 Export composition by factor intensity, 1994 and 2004 (%)

Product category	*China & HK*		*East Asia*		*NAFTA*		*EU*		*WORLD*	
	1994	*2004*	*1994*	*2004*	*1994*	*2004*	*1994*	*2004*	*1994*	*2004*
Non-fuel primary commodities	**7.7**	**4.3**	**6.8**	**4.5**	**15.7**	**12.0**	**14.1**	**11.4**	**14.0**	**11.3**
Labour-intensive and resource-intensive manufactures	**46.4**	**30.9**	**20.7**	**15.2**	**8.1**	**8.4**	**14.9**	**11.7**	**15.3**	**12.4**
Leather, textiles, apparel, and footwear	34.2	21.5	14.5	10.2	2.6	2.6	7.1	5.1	8.6	6.5
Toys and sports equipment	8.3	4.6	2.6	1.9	0.7	0.5	0.5	0.4	1.1	0.8
Wood and paper products	1.7	2.7	2.1	1.9	3.5	3.5	4.5	3.9	3.4	3.2
Non-metallic mineral products	2.2	2.1	1.4	1.2	1.3	1.8	2.8	2.2	2.3	2.0
Low skill-, technology-, capital- and scale-intensive manufactures	**4.9**	**7.5**	**7.5**	**7.8**	**3.4**	**3.8**	**7.5**	**7.2**	**6.6**	**6.8**
Iron and steel	0.7	1.8	2.2	2.8	1.0	1.2	3.5	3.3	2.7	3.0
Fabricated metal products	2.4	3.1	2.1	2.2	1.7	1.9	2.6	2.5	2.2	2.2
Simple transport equipment	0.7	1.3	1.1	1.0	0.3	0.3	0.4	0.5	0.6	0.6
Sanitary and plumbing equipment	0.9	0.9	0.4	0.4	0.2	0.2	0.5	0.4	0.3	0.3
Ships and boats	0.2	0.4	1.7	1.5	0.2	0.2	0.5	0.5	0.8	0.7
Medium skill-, technology-, capital- and scale-intensive manufactures	**11.0**	**15.6**	**24.5**	**23.9**	**30.0**	**29.9**	**29.7**	**30.8**	**25.8**	**26.0**
Rubber and plastic products	2.3	2.2	1.8	1.7	1.4	1.7	2.1	2.0	1.7	1.7
Non-electrical machinery	2.4	4.7	8.9	8.3	11.4	11.2	12.7	12.4	10.5	10.0

(Continued)

Table 2.6 (Continued)

Product category	*China & HK*		*East Asia*		*NAFTA*		*EU*		*WORLD*	
	1994	*2004*	*1994*	*2004*	*1994*	*2004*	*1994*	*2004*	*1994*	*2004*
Electrical machinery other than semiconductors	6.0	8.0	6.3	6.9	5.1	5.5	4.8	4.5	4.9	5.1
Road motor vehicles	0.3	0.7	7.5	7.0	12.2	11.5	10.1	11.8	8.7	9.2
High skill-, technology-, capital- and scale-intensive manufactures	**23.7**	**35.4**	**33.0**	**39.7**	**30.5**	**32.4**	**24.2**	**28.3**	**26.3**	**29.4**
Chemical and pharmaceutical products	3.3	3.4	4.8	6.6	8.3	10.1	12.3	15.6	9.0	11.0
Computers and office equipment	3.9	12.1	8.4	10.0	6.1	5.5	3.5	3.4	4.9	5.0
Communications equipment and semiconductors	11.6	15.9	15.8	18.6	8.3	9.1	3.9	4.8	7.6	8.7
Aircraft	0.1	0.1	0.3	0.2	4.4	3.6	1.8	1.5	1.7	1.4
Scientific instruments, watches and photographic equipment	4.8	3.9	3.7	4.3	3.4	4.2	2.7	3.0	3.1	3.3
Remaining exports	**6.3**	**6.4**	**7.5**	**8.9**	**12.3**	**13.5**	**9.5**	**10.7**	**12.1**	**14.0**

Note: Category definitions from Mayer, Butkevicius and Kadri (2002). Trade between China and Hong Kong not computed in the values presented above. East Asia = emerging East Asia plus Japan.
Source: COMTRADE, SITC Rev. 2. Data reported by member countries.

for an explanation of these categories). The share of labour-intensive exports from China & Hong Kong fell by one-third between 1994 and 2004, while those of low-skill and medium-skill exports increased by the same magnitude and high-skilled exports doubled. These changes were mainly driven by changes in four production networks: computers and office equipment; communications equipment and semi-conductors; electrical machinery other than semi-conductors; and textiles and clothing. Between them, these four sectors account for 57 per cent of China & Hong Kong's exports.

The changing composition of China & Hong Kong's exports is bringing it closer to the composition of exports in the EU and NAFTA and the share of high-skill exports from China & Hong Kong's exceeds that in either the EU or NAFTA. However, one must be careful not to equate the technological classification of a product with the actual technological content of the value added in production performed in the country. For instance, the technological content of designing a chip is much higher than that of manufacturing it, but the trade categorization does not capture this. Hence, the export of higher technological goods does not necessarily imply that a country is involved in the high value-added process of production. In fact, China's process of production tends to be in the lower value-added range (Japanese Ministry of Economy, Trade and Industry, 2005).

The fact that China is both a major exporter and importer of parts and components is a reflection of a growing fragmentation of production by MNCs. Initially, a Japanese producer of TV sets, for example, would manufacture the parts and components at home (or in a NIE) and export the kit to a foreign country to be assembled by an affiliate. The final product would then be either sold in the domestic market, or exported to foreign markets including Japan. The critical factor driving the fragmentation of production was cheaper labour to undertake assembly operations, reduced transport and packaging costs for parts and components trade, and closeness to the customer for local sales of the final product. More recently, the production process is becoming more specialized. The production of individual parts and components has also moved through FDI affiliates to middle-income countries based on their comparative advantage (represented by factor proportions, technological capabilities and industrial infrastructure) so as to achieve a more efficient allocation of production. Such a move was made possible thanks to the recent information and communication technology revolution and the reduction in logistics costs, which allowed firms to link more easily the different subprocesses. (Kawai, 2005).

Figure 2.5 illustrates the evolving structure. Traditionally, parts A and B would be produced in a single advanced country (Japan or the NIEs), and sent for assembly to middle-income East Asian countries. The innovation in the new, more finely specialized production structures is that parts and components manufacturing is also being broken down into design, undertaken in Japan and NIEs, and manufacturing, done in middle-income countries. These individual components are then sent on to Japan/NIEs for quality control, further high value-added processing and grouping into kits, before being returned to middle-income countries for final assembly and then export. This is for instance the structure followed by the Japanese MNC System-Denso which produces air conditioners. The different parts are produced in Thailand, Indonesia and Malaysia and the quality control is performed in Singapore (Asian Development Bank, 2005).

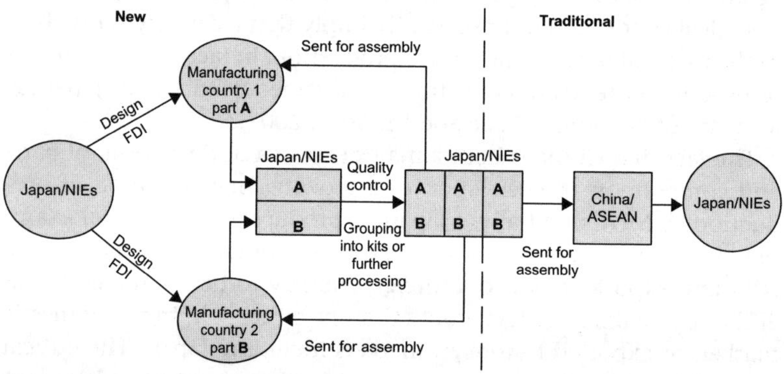

Figure 2.5 Production networks in East Asia: new vs. traditional

The emergence of China as an important exporter of parts and components has forced high-wage economies like Hong Kong, Japan and Singapore to upgrade their own production processes. As Ng and Yeats (2003) report, these economies have adopted a conscious restructuring strategy:

> Partly as a reaction to the East Asian financial crisis, Singapore and Hong Kong adopted a policy of upgrading exports by encouraging

production of high technology products. This strategy relied on increased imports of parts and components, primarily of telecommunications equipment and office machinery, for further assembly (see Lemoine and Unal-Kesenci 2002). In the case of Hong Kong, this strategy drew on the capabilities of 'high technology areas' established within China for the manufacture of technology intensive products. These areas were intended to be counterparts to Silicon Valley in California or the route 128 corridor in Massachusetts. (Ng and Yeats, 2003: 56, 57)

The role of FDI

Regional production networks have been constructed through growing intraregional flows of FDI, creating a mutually reinforcing FDI–trade nexus. As Table 2.7 shows, countries in East Asia have seen high shares of capital coming from other East Asian countries as well as from Japan. China's high share of FDI from the region, as well as the growing share of other middle-income countries, is noteworthy. East Asia's position as a destination for FDI has strengthened over the years, becoming the second-largest FDI recipient in 2004 after the European Union, with over $130 billion received. Major source countries in 2002–04 are Japan ($30.7 billion), Hong Kong ($20.9 billion), Singapore ($6.1 billion) and Taiwan, China ($5.9 billion).

China: an increasing source of FDI

That China has received significant foreign direct investment since the mid 1990s linked to the establishment of processing zones is a

Table 2.7 FDI inflows by origin (% of total)

	US + EU		*Japan*		*Emerging East Asia*	
	1998–00	*2001–03*	*1998–00*	*2001–03*	*1998–00*	*2001–03*
China	20.5	17.8	7.3	8.6	57.8	52.8
Indonesia	24.7	10.9	8.4	6.7	30.8	44.6
Korea	57.6	64.8	11.9	10.5	16.1	11.7
Malaysia	55.9	38.6	20.6	16.4	14.2	23.5
Philippines	39.6	47.0	12.6	30.1	20.2	12.4
Thailand	46.3	−8.8	24.7	42.0	25.6	65.4
Vietnam	31.0	24.5	4.9	6.5	36.1	54.7

Sources: National agencies; registrations or approvals in some cases; World Bank (2004a).

Industry type	*Investor*	*Investment destination*	*Invested company*	*Summary*
Electrical and electronics	Haier	Thailand	Distar Electric Corporation Public Co., Ltd.	Acquires home appliance joint venture plant of Distar and Daewoo Electronics Co., Ltd. and begins consignment production of refrigerators at aforementioned plant, sells refrigerators in Thailand using Distar's sales channel and begins exporting them after 2003
		Japan	Sanyo Electric Co., Ltd.	Begins joint product development with Sanyo; establishes joint venture Sanyo Haier with Sanyo through which it begins selling refrigerators and washing machines from May 2002
	TCL International Holdings Ltd.	Germany	Schneider Electronics GmbH	Acquires production facilities, inventory goods, brand, etc. of bankrupt German TV maker Schneider in September 2002 for approximately 8.2 million euros
		France	Thomson SA	Establishes new joint venture with Thomson, TCL-Thomson Electronics Corporation (TTE), in July 2004; both companies consolidate their TV and DVD manufacturing divisions
	Boe Technology Group Co., Ltd.	Korea	Hydis	Acquires the TFT-LCD* business of Hydis, which is affiliated with Korea's major semiconductor maker Hynix Semiconductor Inc., for US$380 million in January 2003
	Lenovo Group Ltd.	US	IBM	Acquires IBM's personal computer business for US$1.75 billion in November 2004

Automotive	Chery Automobile Co., Ltd.	Iran	SKT	Signs contact to jointly produce passenger vehicles in Iran; production begins in the end of 2003
	Shanghai Automotive Co. Ltd.	Korea	Daewoo Motor Sales Corp.	Acquires 10% of Daewoo's shares, a carmaker affiliated with GM, in October 2002
		Korea	Ssang Yong Motor Company	Acquires Ssang Yong, the fourth largest carmaker in Korea, for 590 billion won in October 2004
	Wanxiang Group Corporation	US	Rockford Powertrain Inc.	Acquires 33.5% of Rockford Powertrain's shares, a well-established US automobile parts maker, in September 2003 and becomes its largest shareholder

Figure 2.6 China's foreign direct investment cases, 2002–04
* Thin Film Transister Liquid Crystal Display.
Source: Ministry of Economy, Trade and Industry (2005).

well-known story. What is a comparatively new story is that China is becoming a source of FDI and is likely to become one of the major sources of FDI in the region (Network China, 2005).

China appears to be taking its upgrading strategy in East Asian production networks one step further. To become less dependent on foreign affiliates, increase the technological capacities of domestic companies and increase control in the production network, Chinese companies are acquiring foreign companies abroad. China's cumulative outward FDI was $38 billion at the end of June 2003. It has increased significantly since and will very likely grow even faster now due to the strengthening of the yuan and accelerating policy moves to facilitate outward FDI (China Network, 2005).

Chinese companies are making overseas acquisitions to acquire technology, brand names, control of distribution networks and have greater proximity to consumers. Figure 2.6 presents some illustrative examples of Chinese companies' recent acquisitions.

Equity market integration in East Asia[3]

If firms are becoming more integrated across East Asia, then it is natural to suppose that equity markets should reflect this fact and also move together. In the last decade, the region's total equity market capitalization (excluding China and Japan) has doubled from approximately US$1,265 billion in 1994 to US$2,309 billion in 2004, despite significant losses at the time of the Asian crisis.[4] Equity markets have also been a notable source of external finance for firms in the region. In the last decade, the total number of firms listed in stockmarkets in East Asia markets have increased by 40 per cent.

Prior to the Asian financial crisis, most equity markets in East Asia were far less developed in terms of their market infrastructures and therefore were relatively segmented, with the exception of Singapore and Hong Kong. Under these conditions, liberalization may not be enough to induce foreign participation in local equity markets (see Bekaert, Harvey and Lundblad, 2003). Informational, regulatory and local economic policy concerns could limit international investors from participation in local equity markets. But as countries in the region become more involved in cross-border real economic activities, the more their equity prices should move together (see, for example Heston and Rouwenhorst, 1994; Brooks and Del Negro, 2003).

One piece of evidence that could suggest greater regional integration in East Asian equity markets is the increase in intra-regional foreign portfolio investment. According to the IMF's Coordinated Portfolio Investment Survey, foreign portfolio investment in both stocks and bonds coming into East Asia has increased from 9 per cent of the region's GDP in 1997 to 14 per cent in 2003. Notably, the share of portfolio investment coming from East Asian NIEs has more than doubled between 1997 and 2003 (Table 2.8).

Another piece of evidence is the increasing co-movement between equity markets in East Asia in recent years, and we look at the correlations between returns in each country and those in the regional market (the weighted average of all other regional countries' returns). We do this for two periods, before and after the Asian financial crisis. As seen from Figure 2.7, the correlation between returns in each East Asian country and the region is high and mostly increasing after the crisis years.[5] Similarly, as seen from Figure 2.8, the correlation between returns in each East Asian country and Japan has increased after the crisis years.

Alternative evidence for regional equity market integration in East Asia is obtained from a news-based test, which focuses on the importance of 'news' (shocks) in explaining the return and volatility of asset prices. We use the same methodology as Baele *et al.* (2004) to measure financial integration in the Euro area. We postulate that the return on equity in any individual country is a function of country-specific news, regional news and global news. Equity markets that are globally integrated would have their returns closely follow global news

Table 2.8 Sources of portfolio investment to East Asia (excluding Japan)

Portfolio investment from (%)	*1997*	*2001*	*2002*	*2003*
United States	41.4	37.0	37.4	37.0
Japan	12.7	6.3	6.6	4.3
European Union	27.3	34.2	28.5	30.9
East Asia NIEs	6.1	13.8	17.4	15.2
Developing East Asia	0.5	0.4	0.4	0.3
Others	15.0	13.4	13.6	15.8
Total	100.0	100.0	100.0	100.0

Source: Staff estimate based on IMF Coordinated Portfolio Investment Survey data.

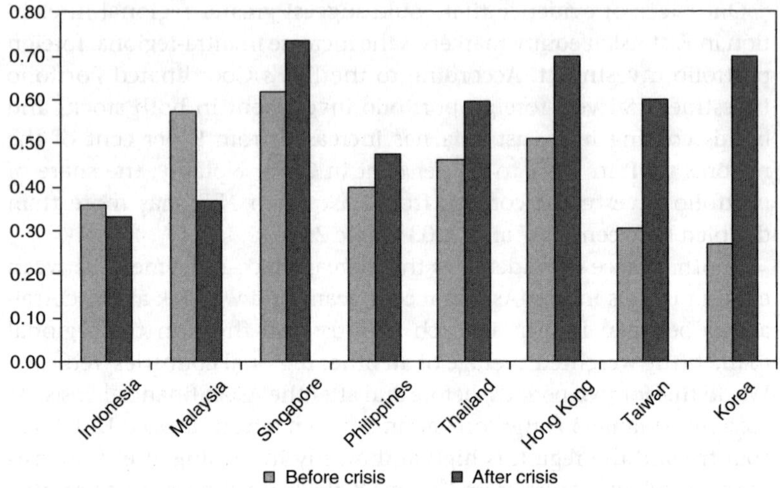

Figure 2.7 Return correlations: country versus region (excluding Japan)
Source: Datastream.

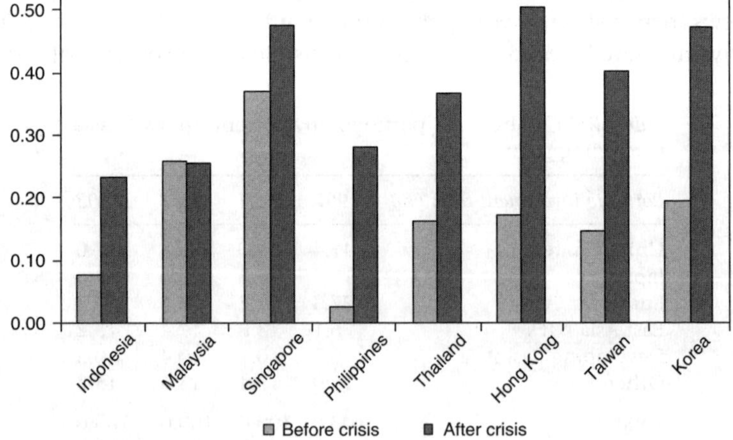

Figure 2.8 Return correlations: country versus Japan
Source: Datastream.

events, while those that are regionally integrated would have returns affected by regional news events.

In order to undertake this analysis, we must first define the country, regional and global news events. We define the news as the residuals from an autoregressive system. Thus, the regional news is given by the actual regional equity return less the 'expected' return, based on the lagged values of the regional equity market. We define the global news in a similar way. The full equation for the country equity return is thus given by the following generalized conditional heteroscedasticity (GARCH) model (the *i* subscript indicates country):

$$\begin{aligned} R_{it} &= \alpha_0 + \alpha_1 Z_{it-1} + \alpha_2 \mu^R_{t-1} + \alpha_3 \mu^J_{t-1} + \alpha_4 \mu^G_{t-1} \\ &\quad + \beta_L e^R_t + \beta_J e^J_t + \beta_G e^G_t + \nu_{it} \end{aligned} \tag{2-4}$$

where R_i is the equity return; Z_i is the set of instruments consisting of lagged local dividend yield and lagged return (country specific effects); μ^R_{t-1}, μ^J_{t-1}, μ^G_{t-1} are the expected regional, Japan, and US (global) return; e^Rt, e^Jt, e^Gt are the regional, Japan and US news defined as residuals from estimating regional, Japan and global equity return separately using GARCH(1,1) model (see Appendix 3 for a more detailed description); and ν_{it} is distributed normally with conditional variance given by:

$$\sigma^2_{\nu,it} = \gamma_0 + \gamma_1 \nu^2_{it-1} + \gamma_2 \sigma^2_{\nu,it-1} + \gamma_3 \zeta^2_{it-1} \tag{2-5}$$

The coefficients (βs) on the residual variables (e), capture the influence of news in the regional, Japanese and US markets respectively. We allow the news coefficient β to take two values, one before and one after the Asian financial crisis. The first test of regional integration is to establish whether the coefficient (β) is significantly different from zero.

A second integration measure is the variance ratio used by Ng (2000) and Beale *et al.* (2004). This measure looks at the proportion of the total variance of equity returns volatility (given by equation (2-5)) explained by the variance of each news component.

We use weekly return data from Datastream (see Appendix 4 for the data source), and the estimation results presented in the Table 2.9 show a strong influence of regional news on domestic equity returns. The size of the coefficients suggests that for some countries the degree of integration is as high as exists in the Euro area, as quoted by Beale *et al.* (2004). The impact of Japan and the USA is also positive, but the

Table 2.9 Estimates of news coefficients in domestic equity return

		Indonesia	*Malaysia*	*Philippines*	*Singapore*	*Thailand*	*Hong Kong*	*Taiwan*	*Korea*
Regional	before crisis	0.485**	0.570**	0.676**	0.499**	0.970**	0.511**	0.505**	0.353*
		(0.064)	(0.060)	(0.078)	(0.048)	(0.078)	(0.052)	(0.102)	(0.081)
	After crisis	0.739**	0.338**	0.575**	0.631**	0.903**	0.558**	0.729**	1.191**
		(0.125)	(0.070)	(0.080)	(0.060)	(0.105)	(0.050)	(0.079)	(0.093)
Wald test: no shift after crisis (*P*-value)		0.070	0.090	0.365	0.090	0.608	0.519	0.080	0.000
Japan	before crisis	0.064	0.201**	0.022	0.209**	0.139*	0.107*	0.175**	0.206**
		(0.045)	(0.035)	(0.057)	(0.029)	(0.054)	(0.050)	(0.054)	(0.066)
	After crisis	0.520**	0.207**	0.249**	0.338**	0.387**	0.314**	0.377**	0.622**
		(0.108)	(0.037)	(0.059)	(0.038)	(0.073)	(0.040)	(0.066)	(0.053)
Wald test: no shift after crisis (*P*-value)		0.000	0.007	0.006	0.007	0.006	0.001	0.018	0.000
USA	before crisis	0.240*	0.451**	0.215*	0.361*	0.328*	0.510*	0.151	0.282*
		(0.086)	(0.059)	(0.085)	(0.049)	(0.110)	(0.072)	(0.150)	(0.121)
	After crisis	0.104	0.151*	0.236**	0.382**	0.381**	0.504**	0.714**	0.627**
		(0.184)	(0.069)	(0.058)	(0.043)	(0.070)	(0.040)	(0.071)	(0.074)
Wald test: no shift after crisis (*P*-value)		0.502	0.743	0.845	0.743	0.685	0.944	0.001	0.015

Note: Before crisis is prior to 01 July 1997, after crisis is after 13 July 1999. ** and * indicate coefficient are statistically significant at 10 and 5 per cent, respectively.
Source: Authors' estimates. Sample period varies for each country. The Bollerslev–Wooldridge consistent standard deviation is shown in parentheses.

magnitude is smaller and the coefficients are not always significantly different from zero. The table also shows that after the Asian crisis, the coefficients for regional news have risen in Indonesia, Singapore, Taiwan, China and Korea. The same phenomenon holds for Japan. The impact of news from US markets, by contrast, has stayed the same except for Taiwan, China and Korea.

The results from the variance ratios show the relative importance of news from different sources (Figure 2.9). In all cases, regional news is more important in determining equity returns than is news from Japan or the USA. For most countries, the regional news dominates, with some 20 per cent or so of the total variance being explained by the variance in regional news. The impact of the USA comes next, followed by Japan. The close integration of Japan and Korea is noteworthy as is the growing integration within the region of both Korea and Taiwan, China. These results are consistent with the view that equity markets in East Asia are becoming more integrated and that

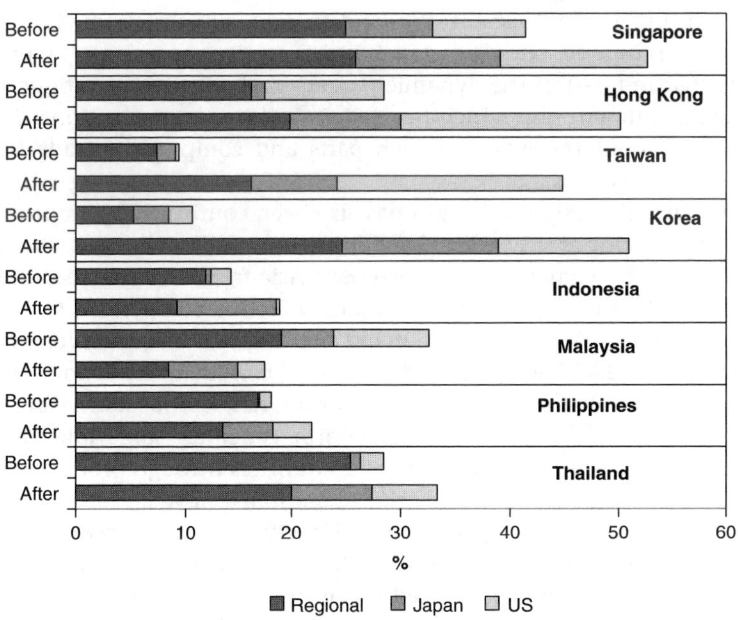

Figure 2.9 Return volatility explained by regional, Japan, and US news

the degree of integration is approaching that of the Euro area for some countries. Conversely, capital control might have caused the decrease in the impact of external news to Malaysian market.

Trade in services integration: an untapped source of great potential for East Asia

East Asia lags behind other developing regions in trade in services and in the openness and integration of their services sectors (Mattoo, Rathindran and Subramanian, 2001). Although recently there has been considerable attention to this issue, and in some areas such as financial services and telecommunications East Asian countries have moved towards more liberal regimes, there is still a general belief that services-sector liberalization has lagged behind liberalization of goods.

This is an anomaly for East Asian development. Services can be construed as a natural by-product of the growing division of labour in production. In a seminal piece in 1984, Bhagwati discusses a process of technical change which can lead services to splinter off from goods, permitting greater specialization and efficiency in the production of these services. He refers to these types of services as technically progressive and part of the dynamic process of change in the economic system, a description which fits well with the previous section's discussion about the way in which parts and components trade has evolved in East Asia.

Bhagwati's analytical insight has also been confirmed by empirical studies looking at the welfare benefits of services liberalization. World Bank (2002) estimates the gains to East Asia from services liberalization at $270 million per year, a figure which is comparable to that generated from full liberalization of trade in goods. In case studies on Thailand and Malaysia, Dee (2004a, 2004b) conducts simulation exercises to show that services liberalization also has very substantial benefits. She concludes that services reform generates some allocative efficiency effects, but largely benefits countries through productivity effects. She finds that the main gains result from unilateral liberalization and that the additional gains from reciprocity in a multilateral context are relatively small. She also finds the welfare gains from unilateral services liberalization to exceed those from unilaterally liberalizing trade in agriculture or manufacturing (Dee, 2004a: 6). In the case of Thailand, the greatest benefits from services liberalization come from trade/distribution and electricity. For Malaysia, similar results hold with the greatest benefits coming from trade and business services. In both cases, the barriers in these sub-sectors tend to be cost-escalating.

Several other studies have documented the benefits to freer services provision. Francois and Schuknecht (2000) examine the link between financial-sector openness and growth and find a strong positive relationship between financial-sector competition and financial-sector openness, and between growth and financial competition. This is supported by Mattoo, Rathindran and Subramanian (2001) who find that countries with fully open telecom and financial sectors grew by up to 1.5 percentage points faster than other countries. Eschenbach and Francois (2002) find that if a 'typical' lower-income country was to move from the openness level characterizing the average lower-income regime to the more liberal openness level characterizing the average higher-income regime (that is, roughly 50 per cent liberalization of financial services trade by these measures), this would imply a difference in growth rates of between roughly 0.4 and 0.6 per cent a year on a per capita basis

Given the evidence in favour of liberalization, and their own experiences with the welfare gains from specialization in goods production and trade, it seems surprising that East Asian countries still maintain significant barriers to services development. Some of these barriers restrict market access broadly, and are as restrictive towards domestic providers as to foreign providers (such as various types of regulation). But other restrictions treat foreigners less favourably than domestic providers: national persons laws that require a physical presence in country to provide services; ownership restrictions on foreigners; minimum capital thresholds for foreigners, or minimum square-footage requirements; business visa requirements; and quota restrictions on branch licensing are some examples of departure from national treatment. And while there is some progress in moving towards liberalization, offers being made in the context of the Doha Round do not offer much hope that substantial services liberalization is high on the development agenda of most East Asian countries. Consequently, services integration, either regionally or with the rest of the world, is lagging behind goods integration in East Asia.

The potential role of India

It is useful to contrast India's performance with that of East Asia in services. A crude comparison of China and India shows that China has a much higher ratio of productivity in manufacturing, compared to average productivity in the economy, than does India (Figure 2.10). Conversely, India has a much higher ratio of productivity in services, compared to average productivity in its economy, than does China. The inference is that China has a comparative advantage in manufacturing production while India has a comparative advantage in services production, which is confirmed in Figure 2.11, which shows India having a revealed comparative advantage in services.

As Panagariya (2004: 36) observes:

> whereas in other countries a decline in the share of agriculture in GDP has been accompanied by a substantial expansion of industry in the early stages of development, in India this has not happened.

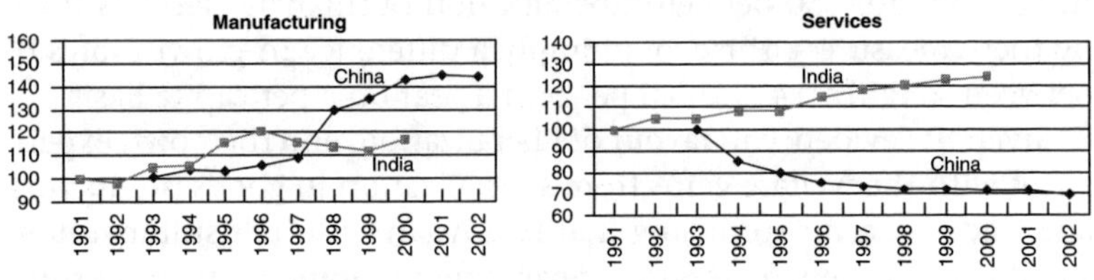

Figure 2.10 Manufacturing and services productivity in China and India
Note: Numbers over 100 mean that manufacturing productivity exceeds overall productivity.
Source: Based on UNCTAD (2005).

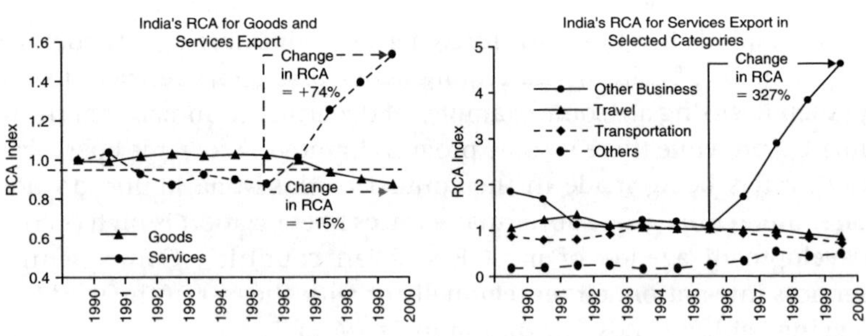

Figure 2.11 India's revealed comparative advantage
Notes: Other business services include software exports, communication, management and consultancy services, construction, news agency services, etc. Other services include insurance and government services.
Source: World Bank (2004b) using IMF's Balance of Payments Statistics data.

Instead, India's emergence as one of the world's fastest growing economies (Virmani, 2005) has been driven by the pace of expansion of its services sector. India's services sector grew by 9 per cent in the 1990s, and its services exports grew by 17 per cent annually. FDI growth in services has outpaced FDI growth in non-services every year since 1992–93, with the gap widening dramatically in 2001–02 when FDI growth in services reached 36 per cent compared to 20 per cent growth in non-services. India's share in world exports of software services reached 17 per cent in 2001, indicating that it is not only growing rapidly but is also a globally important provider (World Bank, 2004).

India's services record is notable because it demonstrates that service sectors can also grow rapidly, with specialization and high export growth, in much the same way as goods sectors have grown. Over time, as India's performance improved, the concentration of its service exports in software and business process outsourcing has increased rapidly. At the same time, the mode of delivery has changed, from custom IT applications to business processing such as data entry, call centres, data conversions and the like. The former are often exported through on-site visits to other countries, and can be affected by regulatory barriers in importing countries such as physical presence requirements. The latter are exported through telecommunications systems and are more affected by the cost of these systems.

Integration with India

One feature of welfare gains from services liberalization is that the bulk of the gains come from unilateral liberalization (because of the productivity growth channel), whereas the bulk of gains from trade liberalization come when undertaken in the context of multilateral agreements (because of market-access benefits). This potentially makes services liberalization easier to achieve than trade liberalization.

Should East Asian countries start to liberalize (and several are already advanced in this direction, including, increasingly, China and Korea), it is natural to suppose that India will become a major exporter of services to these countries. India, in turn, could provide access to a more liberalized goods market that would be of considerable interest to East Asian exporters. Movements in this direction could link two of Asia's fastest growing areas in a mutually advantageous fashion.

Prospects and challenges for East Asia's integration

East Asia's intraregional integration has been accelerating, as evidenced by growing trade, FDI and portfolio links across economies. We argue that this has been largely beneficial for the region as it reflects market forces and has taken place in a context of strong growth and a continued outward orientation with the rest of the world. This kind of integration requires economies to pursue their dynamic comparative advantage and to allocate domestic productive resources efficiently. FDI is also critical, not only because it brings risk capital but also because it brings with it technologies, management know-how, and global brands that encourage the economy to trade (Kawai, 2005).

The development of an FDI-trade nexus within the region is seen in the growing importance of parts and components trade between foreign affiliates. We show that the regional bias is particularly strong in parts and components trade. China is a major new player, both as an importer of parts and components from the rest of the region for assembly and as an efficient exporter of parts and components to other countries. China is also showing signs of emerging as a major source of FDI.

India's integration into the East Asian markets is yet incipient. India's increasing trade with the region still represents a very small share of East Asia's trade. However, India is a major producer and exporter of services, which are relatively undeveloped in East Asia. If East Asian countries opt to pursue services liberalization, the potential for expanding links with India in a mutually beneficial way would expand enormously and it would make good economic sense to include India in regional agreements.

Growing intraregional portfolio capital flows are another sign of regional integration. Much of the variance in the returns in regional equity markets appears to come from common news events, suggesting tight real economy links between countries.

East Asia is still far from the degree of integration of other regions like the EU, especially with regard to monetary integration and harmonization of regulations. But this does not mean that formal regional agreements are required to accelerate the process. Indeed, effective domestic reforms to improve the investment climate, liberalize services, encourage FDI and promote sound domestic capital markets are likely to be most important in furthering regional integration.

Appendix 1: country list

Emerging East Asia: Cambodia, China & Hong Kong, Indonesia, Korea Rep., Lao DPR., Malaysia, Philippines, Singapore, Taiwan (China), Thailand and Vietnam.

East Asia: Emerging East Asia and Japan.

South Asia: Afghanistan, Bangladesh, India, Nepal, Pakistan, and Sri Lanka.

Appendix 2: imports to East Asian Muskats

Though the linearity and normality tests are satisfied for the regressions run for total imports, these tests are not satisfied in some of the regressions for imports of final goods and for imports of parts and components. The regressions for imports of parts and components do not satisfy the linearity test. When outliers are dropped all the regressions for China & Hong Kong satisfy the linearity and normality tests. In the case of Japan some of the regressions satisfy the linearity test once outliers are removed, but not in the case of Korea. We do not experiment with different non-linear functional forms as we wish to maintain comparability with the regressions in final goods, which implies that the results of those regressions should be treated with caution as the coefficients could be biased if the linearity assumption does not hold. The regressions (5) and (6) which are employed to test if the East Asian bias in final goods is statistically different from that in parts and components in 1994 and 2004 satisfy the linearity and normality tests for China & Hong Kong and Japan when the outliers are removed, which leads us to have confidence in their reported results. (See Table 2.10.)

Appendix 3: test for equity market integration

The approach used to test for equity market integration is similar to what Beale *et al.* (2004) and Bekaert *et al.* (2005) have done where each country return is assumed to react to expected component and news. However, this note differs from the previously mentioned study in terms of defining the external factors that drive the expected and unexpected (news) components. Using this approach we can then investigate the degree of integration of equity markets in East Asia towards regional or global markets. The empirical equation for testing the effect of global and regional news on local return is given by the following GARCH(1,1):

$$\begin{aligned} R_{it} &= \alpha_0 + \alpha_1 Z_{it-1} + \alpha_2 \mu^R_{t-1} + \alpha_3 \mu^J_{t-1} + \alpha_4 \mu^G_{t-1} \\ &\quad + \beta_L e^R_t + \beta_J e^J_t + \beta_G e^G_t + \nu_{it} \end{aligned} \tag{A3.1}$$

Table 2.10 Imports to major East Asian markets, 1994 and 2004

	China & Hong Kong					
	Final goods		*Parts & components*		*Final goods and parts and components*	
	(1)	(2)	(3)	(4)	(5)	(6)
Dependent variable	log imports 2004	log imports 1994	log imports 2004	log imports 1994	log imports 2004	log imports 1994
lgdp2004	0.77***		1.99***		0.77***	
	[0.16]		[0.27]		[0.16]	
lgdpcap2004	0.38**		0.29		0.38**	
	[0.18]		[0.35]		[0.18]	
ldist	−0.24	−1.16***	−0.63	−1.45**	−0.24	−1.16***
	[0.34]	[0.37]	[0.57]	[0.60]	[0.35]	[0.37]
lland	0.36**	0.17	−0.37*	0.06	0.36**	0.17
	[0.14]	[0.13]	[0.21]	[0.22]	[0.14]	[0.13]
lgdp1994		0.99***		1.10***		0.99***
		[0.14]		[0.32]		[0.15]
lgdpcap1994		0.31*		1.12***		0.31*
		[0.18]		[0.39]		[0.19]
dummyEA	2.24***	1.48***	2.96***	2.87***	2.24***	1.48***
	[0.60]	[0.55]	[0.95]	[0.80]	[0.61]	[0.56]
dummyEA* dummyP&C					0.72	1.39
					[1.12]	[0.97]
dummyP&C* lgdp2004					1.22***	
					[0.31]	
dummyPC* lgdpcap2004					−0.10	
					[0.39]	
dummyPC*ldist					−0.39	−0.28
					[0.66]	[0.69]
dummyPC*lland					−0.72***	−0.11
					[0.25]	[0.25]
dummyPC* lgdp1994						0.11
						[0.35]
dummyPC* lgdpcap1994						0.81*
						[0.43]
dummy_PC					−25.71***	−16.16**
					[6.97]	[7.32]
Constant	−6.33*	−1.59	−32.04***	−17.76***	−6.33*	−1.59
	[3.77]	[3.64]	[5.94]	[6.45]	[3.80]	[3.67]
Observations	120	120	62	62	182	182
Adjusted R-squared	0.74	0.76	0.82	0.80	0.91	0.90

Notes: Robust standard errors in brackets. * significant at 10%; ** significant at 5%; *** significant at 1%. DummyEA is a dummy with value 1 for East Asian countries. DummyPC is a dummy with value 1 for imports of parts and components.

Table 2.10 (Continued)

	Korea					
	Final goods		*Parts & components*		*Final goods and parts and components*	
Dependent variable	(1) log imports 2004	(2) log imports 1994	(3) log imports 2004	(4) log imports 1994	(5) log imports 2004	(6) log imports 1994
lgdp2004	0.96***		1.51***		0.96***	
	[0.19]		[0.24]		[0.19]	
lgdpcap2004	0.31		0.43		0.31	
	[0.22]		[0.27]		[0.22]	
ldist	−0.15	−0.20	−0.74	−0.91	−0.15	−0.20
	[0.38]	[0.44]	[0.56]	[0.68]	[0.39]	[0.45]
lland	0.27*	0.43***	− 0.33**	− 0.17	0.27*	0.43***
	[0.15]	[0.15]	[0.16]	[0.20]	[0.15]	[0.15]
lgdp1994		0.71***		1.23***		0.71***
		[0.19]		[0.30]		[0.20]
lgdpcap1994		0.54**		1.11***		0.54**
		[0.25]		[0.38]		[0.25]
dummyEA	2.43***	2.53***	2.83***	3.64***	2.43***	2.53***
	[0.64]	[0.74]	[0.65]	[0.84]	[0.64]	[0.75]
dummyEA* dummyP&C					0.40	1.11
					[0.90]	[1.12]
dummyP&C* lgdp2004					0.55*	
					[0.30]	
dummyPC* lgdpcap2004					0.13	
					[0.34]	
dummyPC*ldist					−0.59	−0.72
					[0.67]	[0.81]
dummyPC*lland					−0.59***	−0.60**
					[0.22]	[0.24]
dummyPC* lgdp1994						0.52
						[0.35]
dummyPC* lgdpcap1994						0.57
						[0.45]
dummy_PC					−3.83	−6.06
					[7.20]	[8.54]
Constant	−17.92***	−16.81***	−21.75***	−22.87***	−17.92***	−16.81***
	[3.73]	[4.14]	[6.24]	[7.57]	[3.76]	[4.18]
Observations	131	131	66	66	197	197
Adjusted R–squared	0.72	0.64	0.78	0.77	0.75	0.72

Notes: Robust standard errors in brackets. * significant at 10%; ** significant at 5%; *** significant at 1%. DummyEA is a dummy with value 1 for East Asian countries. DummyPC is a dummy with value 1 for imports of parts and components.

(Continued)

Table 2.10 (Continued)

	Japan					
	Final goods		*Parts & components*		*Final goods and parts and components*	
Dependent variable	(1) log imports 2004	(2) log imports 1994	(3) log imports 2004	(4) log imports 1994	(5) log imports 2004	(6) log imports 1994
lgdp2004	0.80***		1.37***		0.80***	
	[0.16]		[0.26]		[0.16]	
lgdpcap2004	0.49***		0.52*		0.49***	
	[0.16]		[0.28]		[0.16]	
ldist	0.31	0.31	−1.42***	−1.57***	0.31	0.31
	[0.40]	[0.43]	[0.39]	[0.41]	[0.40]	[0.43]
lland	0.28**	0.38***	−0.23	−0.29	0.28**	0.38***
	[0.12]	[0.12]	[0.20]	[0.19]	[0.12]	[0.12]
lgdp1994		0.68***		1.13***		0.68***
		[0.17]		[0.26]		[0.17]
lgdpcap1994		0.54***		0.69**		0.54***
		[0.16]		[0.28]		[0.16]
dummyEA	3.37***	3.21***	3.38***	3.52***	3.37***	3.21***
	[0.51]	[0.70]	[0.94]	[0.90]	[0.51]	[0.70]
dummyEA* dummyP&C					0.01	0.31
					[1.07]	[1.14]
dummyP&C* lgdp2004					0.57*	
					[0.30]	
dummyPC* lgdpcap2004					0.03	
					[0.32]	
dummyPC*ldist					−1.73***	−1.89***
					[0.56]	[0.59]
dummyPC*lland					−0.51**	−0.67***
					[0.23]	[0.23]
dummyPC* lgdp1994						0.45
						[0.31]
dummyPC* lgdpcap1994						0.15
						[0.32]
dummy_PC					4.71	9.93
					[6.51]	[7.24]
Constant	−18.88****	−18.01***	−14.18***	−8.08***	−18.88***	−18.01***
	[4.42]	[4.84]	[4.77]	[5.39]	[4.42]	[4.84]
Observations	79	79	79	79	158	158
Adjusted R-squared	0.83	0.81	0.76	0.73	0.84	0.84

Notes: Robust standard errors in brackets. * significant at 10%; ** significant at 5%; *** significant at 1%. DummyEA is a dummy with value 1 for East Asian countries. DummyPC is a dummy with value 1 for imports of parts and components.

where R_i is equity return of country i, Z_i is the set of instrument consist of lagged local dividend yield and lagged return, μ^G_{t-1} and μ^R_{t-1} are the global and regional excess return as described in Bekaert *et al.* (2005), e^G_t and e^R_t are global and the regional shocks, ν_{it} ~N(0, σ2ν, it) with conditional variance of:

$$\sigma^2_{\nu,it} = \gamma_0 + \gamma_1 \nu^2_{it-1} + \gamma_2 \sigma^2_{\nu,it-1} + \gamma_3 \zeta^2_{it-1} \qquad \text{(A3.2)}$$

The last component of equation (A3-2) is $\xi_{it} = \min(\nu_{it}, 0)$ captures the asymmetric responses in away that a past negative shock causes higher volatility.

We use two steps for estimating coefficients in equation (A3-1) and (A3-2). First we estimate the global, Japan and regional return equations separately using GARCH(1,1) model to obtain their expected returns based on past information (μ_{t-1}) and residuals (e_t). For the global (US) return model, we include the following instruments: lagged return, lagged spread between 3-month Treasury Bill and 3-month euro–dollar rates, lagged spread between 3-month Treasury Bill and 10-years Treasury Bond rates, lagged changes in 3-month Treasury Bill rate, and lagged dividend yield. For Japan and regional equity returns, the following instruments are used: lagged return, lagged dividend yield; and the expected US return at $t-1$ or μ^G_{t-1}. The second step we estimate equation (A3-1) and (A3-2).

The first integration measure is the coefficient β of equation (A3-1), which directly measures the volatility spillover, that is the intensity of regional and global news to domestic equity return. In equation (A3-1), we use dummy variables to allow the parameter to shift before and after the financial crisis. The β is therefore defined as $\beta = \beta\text{prior} + Ic^*\beta\text{crisis} + Ip^*\beta\text{after}$, where *Ic* and *Ip* is the crisis and after-crisis dummy variable. The significance dummy variable in shifting the parameter after crisis in shifting β is tested using the Wald test.

The second integration measure is the variance ratio used by Ng (2000) and Beale *et al.* (2004). The ratio captures the proportion of volatility in domestic equity return explained by regional or global shock. The ratio is obtained by first computing the return volatility, that is the total variance of the news component of domestic return from equation (A3-1):

$$\sigma^2_{it} = \left(\beta_R e^R_t\right)^2 + \left(\beta_J e^J_t\right)^2 + \left(\beta_G e^G_t\right)^2 + \sigma^2_{\nu,it} \qquad \text{(A3-3)}$$

The global and regional variance ratios are the proportion of variance of domestic return innovation explained by global, Japan or regional news:

$$VR^G_{it} = \frac{\left(\beta_G e^G_t\right)^2}{\sigma^2_{it}}, \; VR^J_{it} = \frac{\left(\beta_J e^J_t\right)^2}{\sigma^2_{it}} \text{ and } VR^R_{it} = \frac{\left(\beta_R e^R_t\right)^2}{\sigma^2_{it}}$$

Table 2.11 Data characteristics (equity return)

	ID	*MY*	*SG*	*PH*	*TH*	*HK*	*TW*	*KO*	*JP*	*USA*
Mean	−0.12	0.09	0.10	0.04	0.07	0.26	−0.02	0.08	0.01	0.21
Median	0.12	0.13	0.15	−0.09	−0.01	0.39	0.22	0.05	0.04	0.40
Max	33.57	30.30	12.31	23.48	43.09	18.33	18.23	25.33	15.66	12.34
Min	−37.91	−33.76	−13.92	−22.41	−21.37	−29.11	−27.56	−44.24	−12.25	−11.74
Std. dev.	6.17	4.54	3.04	4.30	5.38	3.82	4.63	5.47	3.24	2.28
Skewness	−0.295	−0.117	−0.284	0.051	0.650	−0.629	−0.556	−0.472	0.244	−0.251
Kurtosis	10.38	15.56	6.11	6.58	9.98	9.31	5.69	9.90	4.53	5.94
Number of observations	795	1016	1330	868	964	1330	895	928	1330	1330

Note: ID = Indonesia, MY = Malaysia, SG = Singapore, PH = Philippines, TH = Thailand, HK = Hong Kong SAR, KO = S. Korea, JP = Japan, USA = United States.

Appendix 4: data source for testing equity market integration

We use the weekly dividend-adjusted return index and market values provided by Thomson Datastream. The data for equity return indices and market value are in US$ and the return is obtained by taking differences in logs of the return index.

The regional equity return for a particular country is obtained from the weighted return of countries in the East Asia region excluding the country in focus and Japan:

$$R_{it}^{L} = \frac{\sum_{j \notin i} \left(V_t^j . R_t^j \right)}{\sum_{j \notin i} V_t^j}$$

where i = (Indonesia, Malaysia, Singapore, Philippines, Hong Kong, Thailand, Taiwan and South Korea) (Table 2.11).

Notes

1 Emerging East Asia is defined here as ASEAN plus China & Hong Kong, plus Taiwan, China, plus South Korea. Myanmar and Brunei are not included due to lack of data. Country groupings are defined in Appendix 1.
2 These numbers differ from those quoted by the Asian Development Bank (ADB) and others because we do not include China–Hong Kong trade as intra-regional.
3 This section draws from the forthcoming financial sector flagship report of the East Asia and Pacific PREM Department of the World Bank.
4 Source: World Federation of Exchanges. Markets included: Indonesia (Jakarta Stock Exchange), Malaysia (Bursa Malaysia), Singapore (Singapore Stock Exchange), Philippines (Manila Stock Exchange), Thailand, Hong-Kong SAR, Taiwan, and South Korea.
5 Here the Asian financial crisis is defined as period from 1 July 1997 to 13 July 1999.

References

Asian Development Bank (2005) *Asian Economic Cooperation and Integration: Progress, Prospects, and Challenges*.

Ando, M. and F. Kimura (2003) 'The Formation of International Production and Distribution Networks in East Asia', NBER Working Paper Series 10167, December.

Athukorala, P. and N. Yamashita (2005) 'Production Fragmentation and Trade Integration: East Asia in a Global Context', ANU Working Papers in Trade and Development 2005. Available at http://rspas.anu.edu.au/economics/publish/papers/ wp2005/wp-econ-2005-07.pdf.

Bhagwati, J. (1984) 'Splintering and Disembodiment of Services and developing Nations', *The World Economy*, June.

Batra, A. (2004) 'India's Global Trade Potential: The Gravity Model Approach', Indian Council for Research on International Economic Relations. New Delhi, India.

Beale, L., A. Ferrando, P. Hördahl, E. Krylova and C. Monnet (2004) 'Measuring Financial Integration in the Euro Area', European Central Bank, occasional paper series no.14, April.

Bekaert, G., C. R. Harvey and C. T. Lundblad (2003) 'Equity Market Liberalization in Emerging Markets' *Journal of Financial Research*, vol. 26, no. 3, pp. 275–99.

Bekaert, G., C.R. Harvey, and A. Ng. (2005) 'Market Integration and Contagion', *Journal of Business*, vol. 78, no. 1, pp. 39–69.

Brooks, R. and M. Del Negro (2003) 'Country Versus Region Effects in International Stock Returns', Federal Reserve Bank of Atlanta, Working Paper no. 2002-20a.

Brouwer, Gordon de. (2003) 'Financial Markets, Institutions, and Integration in East Asia', *Asian Economic Papers*, 2:1 pp 53–80.

Dee, P. (2004a) 'Cost of Services Trade Restrictions in Thailand', background report of the 'Productivity and Investment Climate Assessment in Thailand'. A World Bank Study for the National Economic and Social Development Board (NESDB), in collaboration with the Foundation for Thailand Productivity Institute (FTPI) Poverty Reduction, Economic Management and Financial Sector Unit (PREM) Washington, DC.

— (2004b) 'Measuring the Cost of Regulatory Restrictions on Services Trade in Malaysia' A background report to the Study on 'Improving the investment Climate by Reducing the Regulatory Burden in Malaysia', a World Bank Study for the Economic Planning Unit (EPU), Malaysia, Poverty Reduction, Economic Management and Financial Sector Unit (PREM), East Asia and Pacific Region, Washington, DC.

Eichengreen, B., Y. Rhee, and H. Tong (2004) 'The impact of China on the Exports of Other Asian Countries', NBER Working Paper No. 10768. National Bureau of Economic Research. Cambridge, Mass.

Eschenbach, F., and J. F. Francois (2002) 'Financial Sector Competition, Services Trade, and Growth', CEPR Discussion Paper No. 3573.

Frankel, J. A., E. Stein and S. -J. Wei (1997) 'Continental Trading Blocks: Are they Natural or Supernatural?' in Jeffrey A. Frankel (ed.), *The Regionalization of the World Economy*, University of Chicago Press, Chicago and London, pp. 91–120.

Frankel, Jeffrey A. and Shang-Jin, Wei (1993) 'Trade Blocs and Currency Blocs' (1993-04-01). NBER Working Paper No. W4335. Available at SSRN: http://ssrn.com/abstract=227026.

Francois, J. F., and L. Schuknecht (2002) 'International Trade in Financial Services, Competition, and Growth Performance', CIES Working Paper No. 6.

Gaulier, G., F. Lemoine and D. Unal-Kesenci (2005) 'China's Integration in East Asia: Production Sharing, FDI & High-Tech Trade', Working Papers 2005-09, CEPII Research Centre.

Heston, S. L., and K. Geert Rouwenhorst (1994) 'Does Industrial Structure Explain the Benefits of International Diversification?', *Journal of Financial Economics,* no. 36, pp. 3–27.

Hummels, D. (1999) 'Have International Transportation Costs Declined?', University of Chicago, Chicago, IL

Japanese Ministry of Economy, Trade and Industry (2005) White Paper on International Economy and Trade 2005, Overview: Towards a New Dimension of Economic Prosperity in Japan and East Asia, Japan. http://www.meti.go.jp/english/report/data/gIT05maine.html.

Kawai, M. (2005) 'East Asian Economic Regionalism: Progress and Challenges', *Journal of Asian Economics*, vol. 16, pp. 29–55.

Kawai, M., and S. Urata (2004) 'Trade and Foreign Direct Investment in East Asia', in: *Economic Linkages and Implications for Exchange Rate Regimes in East Asia*, edited by G. de Brouwer and M. Kawai, 15–102. London and New York: Routledge Curzon.

Lemoine, F. and D. Unal-Kesenci (2002) 'China in the International Segmentation of Production Processes' Paris, Centre d'Etudes Prospectives et al. Information Working Paper 2002–02, March.

Mattoo, A., R. Rathindran and A. Subramanian (2001) 'Measuring Services Trade Liberalization and its Impact on Economic Growth: An Illustration' World Bank Policy Research Working Paper No. 2655.

Mayer, J., A. Butkevicius, and A. Kadri (2002) 'Dynamic Products in World Exports', UNCTD. Discussion Papers No. 159. United Nations Conference on Trade and Development. Geneva, Switzerland.

Network China (2005) 'China: World's Next Big Source of FDI', http://networkchina.iesingapore.com/cnn/news/index.cfm?fuseaction=viewContent&Cat=10&ID=1005&viewmonth=9-2005.

Ng, A. (2000) 'Volatility Spillover Effects from Japan and the US to the Pacific-Basin', *Journal of International Money and Finance*, vol. 19, pp. 207–233.

Ng, F. and A. Yeats (2003) 'Major Trade Trends in East Asia: What Are Their Implications for Regional Cooperation and Growth?', Policy Research Working Paper 3084. World Bank, Washington, DC.

Panagariya, A. (2004) 'India's Trade Reform', *India Policy Forum*, xxvi, pp. 1–67.

Rajan, R. (2004) 'FDI, Trade and the Internationalization of Production in the Asia-Pacific Region: Issues and Policy Conundrums', NUS Working Paper SPP-01-05. Available at http://www.spp.nus.edu.sg/docs/wp/wp0501b.pdf.

Rose, A. (2004) 'Do we Really Know that the WTO Increases Trade?', *American Economic Review*, vol. 94. 1: 98–114.

Virmani, A. (2005) 'A Tripolar Century: USA, China, and India', ICRIER working paper no. 160.

World Bank (2002) *Global Economic Prospects: Making Trade Work for the World's Poor*. Washington, DC.

— (2003) *East Asia Integrates*. Homi Kharas and Kathie Krum (eds). Washington, DC, pp. 1–264.

— (2004a) East Asia and Pacific Regional Brief. Poverty Reduction Economic Management. East Asia and Pacific Region, April. Washington, DC.

— (2004b) *Sustaining India's Services Revolution: Access to Foreign Markets, Domestic Reform and International Negotiations*, chapter 1 'The Remarkable Dynamism of India's Services Sector', Washington DC, pp. 1–60.

3

The Relationship between China and India within the Framework of Asian Economic Integration

Zhang Yuyan

Introduction

For numerous historical, political and economic reasons, economic relations between China and India have been at a standstill for a long time. With the deepening of Asian economic integration and the rapid economic development of both countries, Sino-Indian relations have been put on the global agenda. Strengthened Sino-Indian cooperation would bring a wide range of common benefits to both countries, but nonetheless various factors restrict the two countries in the development of further cooperation. This chapter argues that China and India have ended their long history of self-imposed isolation from each other and that cooperation between the two countries can and should be expected to develop progressively and continually. However, the depth and extent of the cooperation should generally be termed as 'being good neighbours', in that China and India will cooperate at regional and international levels and on specific issues. Generally speaking, the likelihood is not great that, in the short term, China and India will establish a bilateral free-trade area or form an overall strategic alliance within the most probable global scenario.

Regional economic integration is undergoing an unprecedented boom, and according to World Trade Organization (WTO) statistics, by July 2005 the total number of regional trade agreements (RTAs) had exceeded 180 worldwide and, discounting some overlapping areas within these, there are 138 RTAs playing an active role. In Europe, the Maastricht Treaty officially took effect in 1993, creating the European Union (EU), the highest-level institutionalized organization for economic integration so far. On 1 May 2004, the entry of 10 new members expanded the EU to 25 member states. In the Americas, there is the North American Free Trade Agreement (NAFTA) in the North, and the Southern Common Market (Mercosur) and the Andean Community in the South. On the basis of these organizations, preliminary discussions for setting up the Free Trade Area of the Americas (FTAA), encompassing 34 members, have taken place with the vigorous promotion of the United States. Since the late 1990s, the process of Asian economic integration has also increasingly developed, with the Association of South-East Asian Nations (ASEAN) being the central hub, and ASEAN + 1 and ASEAN + 3 being two main supporting pillars.

The process of economic integration is one of continuous reduction of transaction costs between members in order to bring about increased gains from trade through the progressive expansion of the scope and scale of the market, and to achieve other non-trade benefits through the unification and extension of institutions. Although increased costs may be brought about by increased numbers of members, 'free-riding' problems, and greater distances in the process of global economic integration, nonetheless, regional economic integration can bring about the benefits of integration in an even more concentrated way. For instance, among constituent members, even closer economic connections can be established, more trade generated and concomitant benefits obtained. Furthermore, the bargaining strength of the collective members can be enhanced in the negotiation of international rules as in the WTO. Since the 1990s, regional economic integration has been prospering worldwide. Meanwhile, such political and economic factors as conflicts of interest between domestic groups, competition between nation states, and external pressures still restrict the depth and scope of such integration. The development of regional integration is changing the overall pattern of traditional relations between countries and is reshaping the state of the world today.

Asia is a latecomer in regional integration. However, its integration has been accelerating at multiple levels. During this process, the economic relationship between China and India – two countries that have experienced similar aftereffects of colonialism in their history, that are opening up their economies through similar reforms at present, and that share long geographical borders – is attracting greater attention around the world. This process will not only affect the two countries themselves, but will also have a great impact on the regional integration process in Asia and even on future global international relations. This chapter attempts to throw light on the incentives for and impediments to closer economic relations between the two countries and, on this basis, to outline the prospects for Sino-Indian economic relations.

The remainder of the chapter is organized as follows. The next section discusses the benefits and costs of economic integration as well as the progress of integration in Asia. The history and current status of Sino-Indian relations is then introduced, before the incentives for and impediments to Sino-Indian cooperation in the new context are analysed. Finally, the prospects for Sino-Indian relations are considered in the concluding section.

Development of economic integration in Asia

Economic integration is the collective action that allows the enlargement of the scale and scope of the market, with the concomitant unification and extension of rules and institutions. The result is increasingly close economic connections between members.

Benefits and costs of economic integration

There are many potential benefits of integration generated from the enlargement of the scale of the market and unification of the rules and institutions. As far as the scale and scope of the market – that is, the depth and extent of exchange – is concerned, economic integration helps in realizing potential gains from trade based on each member's respective advantages; promoting members' economic growth through deepening the division of labour; and enabling enterprises to realize economies of scale.

As far as the unification and extension of internal rules and institutions among members is concerned, economic integration is firstly conducive to decreased transaction costs.[1] Market segmentation results in various transaction costs, which include tariff and non-tariff barriers, non-free movement of capital and labour, currency-conversion risks, and other costs arising from the differences in rules and extent of enforcement among members. Economic integration can internalize external transactions, thus hugely decreasing transaction costs. Speaking from an even broader perspective of institutions (Zhang Yuyan, 1992), the unification of the 'rules of the game' contributes to providing information to each member, stabilizing expectations and encouraging members to cooperate. A good example in this respect is the effect of integration on national security. Because integration signals that the country will adhere to opening-up and reform, other countries will have greater confidence in that country.[2]

Global economic integration is the realization of economic integration on a worldwide scale, while regional integration is confined to a smaller geographical area. While global economic integration is still moving ahead, regional economic integration, being an alternative and supplement to globalization, has also been flourishing since the 1990s, changing the traditional relations between countries, and reshaping the state of the world today.

The reasons for the rapid development of regional integration include, first of all, the **costs** that global economic integration entails. The costs of economic globalization mainly find expression in three aspects: (a) any integration has an optimal scale on which marginal benefits equal marginal costs. On the one hand, integration reduces the transaction costs resulting from market segmentation, while on the other hand the expansion of the scale of integration also increases internal transaction costs.[3] Thus, the development of integration is often confined within a certain scale. (b) In the supply of global public goods there are 'free-riding' problems which increase the cost of global economic integration (Olson, 1965). However, being in the nature of 'club goods', regional economic integration can partially overcome such problems through providing exclusive club goods. (c) Lastly, there is the cost generated from greater distances. Although technological progress hugely shortens space-time distances, the problem of distance does not fully disappear, and thus transportation costs and costs arising from cultural differences are still factors limiting the division of labour. Due to the fact that regional economic integration has relatively low transportation and cultural costs, it can be achieved relatively easily compared to global integration.

Secondly, regional economic integration can bring member countries more concentrated **regional benefits** compared to non-member countries. Even closer economic connections can be established among member countries through eliminating tariff barriers and lowering non-tariff barriers; more trade and a greater variety of trade benefits can be obtained; and, furthermore, the strength of collective bargaining can be enhanced in the negotiation of international rules such as with the WTO. As far as the formulation of international rules is concerned, currently the 'rules of the game' for globalization are mainly under the control of the developed countries. The relative development of emerging markets makes the establishment of new rules necessary. In order to increase bargaining strength, the major powers strive to consolidate and enlarge their sphere of influence, establishing rules that benefit themselves within the region and hinder competition outside the region. In this process, some countries take the lead in forming economic integration organizations, while other countries respond by doing likewise due to their fear of being excluded from the benefits.

Thirdly, some forms of regional integration are generated in special historical contexts, featuring **path dependency**. The origin of the European Coal and Steel Community (ECSC) in 1951 was fundamentally political – namely, a desire to prevent yet another European war between France and Germany – while the establishment of ASEAN in 1967 was a product of the Cold War. Since then, these non-economic organizations have developed into economic integration organizations – that is to say, there has been a 'spillover effect' from political cooperation to economic cooperation.

Despite the benefits of integration, it is worth noting that the development of economic integration in reality does not always run smoothly. There are various political and economic factors that hamper the development of economic integration.

Domestically speaking, there are conflicts of interest among groups. Since the benefits of free trade are not distributed equally, some groups gain and some groups lose, absolutely or relatively. As a result, the groups that benefit most are often those with the greatest enthusiasm to push liberalization further, such as multinationals and trade sectors. Those interest groups that lose out may hamper the process of integration. The struggle among domestic interest groups often brings high political costs to integration.

Internationally, there is competition among nation-states. To some extent, economic integration requires that member countries cede part of their sovereignty in order to integrate. However, the main structural unit in today's international community is still the nation-state, and globalization does not eliminate such national interests. To a large extent, nation-states strengthen their national interests by virtue of globalization, and they have their own identities, which gives them a distinct role in the global arena. Thus, competition between nation-states also hampers the realization of the common interests deriving from integration.

Moreover, external pressures also have an impact on the degree of integration. Positively speaking, a common sense of identity can be strengthened within a regional grouping in order to protect its members' common interests when there is considerable external pressure. The larger such external pressure, the greater the motivation to integrate, and conversely. Negatively speaking, integration among relatively weak or competing countries may be vulnerable to the external pressure of big powers.

To a large extent, the process of regional integration is the process of achieving common benefits through continuously overcoming political and economic barriers.

Development of Asian economic integration

Compared with Europe and the Americas, Asia[4] is a latecomer in regional economic integration. The importance of sovereignty resulting from a history of colonialism and the Cold War confined the development of regional integration. In recent years, however, the aforesaid factors promoting regional integration have also manifested themselves in Asia. As the opportunity cost of not integrating increased, Asia rapidly strengthened economic ties and established free-trade areas. Asia, as a whole, is forming its own identity in parallel with those of the Americas and Europe.

Currently, East Asia has the highest degree of regional integration in Asia. After the Japan-led 'flying-geese' model of production,[5] East Asia is forming new regional production chains and networks based on a horizontal division of labour, with China at the core of assembly work, and the final products being exported to the global market. This production chain has increased the intra-regional trade in components and parts, especially with information technology (IT) products. What is more, in recent years, with the increase of domestic demand in East Asian countries, intra-regional demand has risen still further for products other than IT goods, making for even more mature integration in East Asia. According to Kawai (2005), by 2003, intra-regional trade accounted for 54 per cent of total trade in East Asia, while intra-regional trade made up 64.4 per cent of EU trade and 46 per cent of NAFTA trade. Measured by the trade-intensity index, East Asia's intra-regional trade intensity index was 2.2, which was higher than the EU figure of 1.7 but slightly lower than the NAFTA figure of 2.5. Both sets of figures would indicate that trade integration is relatively high in East Asia.[6]

Compared with East Asia, the degree of integration in South Asia is much more moderate; intra-regional trade accounts for only 4 per cent of its total exports (Table 3.1). The main reason is that India, as

Table 3.1 Exports of trade groupings

Intra-regional trade as % of total exports and total 2002 exports in millions of US$

Trade grouping	*Date of creation*	*1970*	*1980*	*1990*	*2002*	*Total exports 2002*
Americas						
Andean Community	1996	1.8	3.8	4.1	10.6	5,673
Central American Common Market	1960	26.0	24.4	15.3	11.5	2,598
Caribbean Community	1973	4.2	5.3	8.1	13.5	1,276
Free Trade Area of the Americas	1994	45.0	43.4	46.6	60.7	788,114
Latin American Integration Association	1980	9.9	13.9	11.6	13.6	43,094
Southern Common Market	1994	9.4	11.6	8.9	17.7	16,544
North American Free Trade Agreement	1992	36.0	33.6	41.4	56.0	612,965
Asia						
Association of South East Asian Nations	1967	22.4	17.4	19.0	22.8	94,760
Bangkok Agreement	1975	2.8	1.7	1.6	7.4	44,470
South Asian Association for Regional Cooperation	1985	3.2	4.8	3.2	3.9	2,697
Europe						
European Community (EU)	1957 (1992)	59.5	60.8	65.9	61.0	1,469,856

Source: UNCTAD data.

a great power in South Asia, has very limited trade with other countries in the region.

In the institutional construction of economic integration, unlike in the Americas and Europe where regional integration was dominated by giant powers or core countries, Asia – due to the lack of a power with an absolute advantage – is attempting to ultimately build widespread regional integration through multilevel integration, including at regional, subregional and bilateral levels. At the regional level of cooperation proposed by India in 2004, Asia has been considering the establishment of an Asian Economic Community similar to the EU. Bilateral free-trade agreements are also thriving (Table 3.2). At the subregional level, some integration organizations have been established in Southeast Asia, East Asia and South Asia; these subregions would then be combined into a bigger Asian integration 'road map'.

In Southeast Asia, the ASEAN Free Trade Area (AFTA) has been in effect among the original five ASEAN members since January 2002. It is expected to eliminate tariffs and realize free trade within the entire region by 2015. To move further, in 2003 ASEAN leaders agreed to establish an ASEAN Economic Community, a single market and production base with a free flow of goods, services, investment, capital and skilled labour, by 2020. In East Asia, ASEAN, as the hub, was joined by China, Japan and South Korea to form ASEAN + 3 and (the original) ASEAN + 1, thus forming two parallel mechanisms for integration. ASEAN + 3 was institutionalized in 1997, and since then cooperation on trade, finance, agricultural, information and energy cooperation has been strengthened. In 2004, the ASEAN summit proposed the establishment of an East Asian Economic Community (EAEC), signalling a new stage of East Asian cooperation. At the same time, ASEAN has conducted separate bilateral negotiations with China, Japan and South Korea within the framework of ASEAN + 1. China signed the Framework Agreement on Comprehensive Economic Cooperation with ASEAN in 2002, aimed at completing a free-trade agreement (FTA) by 2010 for the ASEAN-6 members and by 2015 for the CLMV countries (Cambodia, Laos, Myanmar and Vietnam). In order to accelerate the process, an 'early harvest' system has been implemented since 2004, involving the rapid reduction of tariffs on a number of products, mainly agricultural. Then Japan and ASEAN agreed on an economic partnership agreement (EPA) with a view to achieving free trade by 2012 (including allowing an additional five

Table 3.2 Recently established or proposed FTAs in Asia, 1999–2004

Country/ Grouping	*Partners*	*Status of Agreement, 2004*	*Country/Grouping*	*Partners*	*Status of Agreement, 2004*
ASEAN	China	Framework agreement signed	**Malaysia**	China	Under negotiation
	India	Framework agreement signed		Japan	Under negotiation
	Japan	Framework agreement signed		USA	Proposed
	South Korea	Under study			
	USA (TIFA)	Under negotiation			
	CER*	Under study			
	ASEAN+3	Under study			
	EU	Proposed			
China (mainland)	ASEAN	Agreement signed	**Philippines**	China	Under negotiation
	Australia	Proposed		Japan	Under negotiation
	India	Under study		USA	Proposed
	Hong Kong	Agreement signed			
	Macau	Proposed			
	Malaysia	Under negotiation			
	New Zealand	Proposed			
	Thailand	Under negotiation			
	Singapore	Proposed			

(*Continued*)

Table 3.2 (Continued)

Country/ Grouping	*Partners*	*Status of Agreement, 2004*	*Country/Grouping*	*Partners*	*Status of Agreement, 2004*
India	ASEAN	Framework agreement signed	**Singapore**	Australia	Agreement in force
				Canada	Under negotiation
	China	Proposed		China	Proposed
	South Korea	Proposed		Egypt	Proposed
	Singapore	Under negotiation		EFTA	Agreement in force
	Sri Lanka	Agreement in force		EU	Proposed (rejected by EU)
	Thailand	Agreement in force		India	Under negotiation
	BIMSTEC	Framework agreement signed		Japan	Agreement in force
				Jordan	Agreement in force
	SACU	Proposed		Korea	Under negotiations
	COMESA	Proposed		Mexico	Under negotiations
	Southern Common Market	Framework agreement signed		New Zealand	Agreement in force
				Sri Lanka	Under negotiation
	Mauritius	Under negotiation			
	GCC	Proposed		Pakistan	Proposed
	Chile	Proposed		USA	Agreement in force
	SAARC/SAFTA	Agreement in force		Panama	Proposed
				Pacific Three (P-3) (New Zealand, Singapore and Chile)	Under negotiation

Japan	ASEAN	Framework Agreement	**Thailand**	Australia	Agreement signed
	Canada	signed		Bahrain	Agreement signed
	Chile	Proposed		China	Agreement signed
	Korea	Under study		India	Agreement in force
	Malaysia	Under study		Japan	Under negotiation
	Mexico	Under negotiation		Korea	Under study
	Philippines	Under negotiation		New Zealand	Under study
	Singapore	Under negotiation		Peru	Agreement signed
	Thailand	Agreement in force		South Africa	Under study
	Australia	Under negotiation		USA	Under negotiation
		proposed			
Korea	Australia	Under study			
	China	Under study			
	Chile	Agreement signed			
	Japan	Under study			
	Mexico	Under negotiation			
	Peru	Proposed			
	New Zealand	Under study			
	Singapore	Under negotiation			
	Thailand	Under study			
	USA	Under negotiation			

*CER refers to Australia – New Zealand Closer Economic Relation.
Source: Rajan and Sen (2004).

years for the CLMV countries), with due consideration given to the level of economic development and the sensitivity of various sectors within each country. South Korea is also considering similar negotiations with ASEAN, aiming at achieving a high level of trade liberalization, with at least 80 per cent of products having zero tariffs by 2009, and with consideration for special and differential treatment and additional flexibility for the newer ASEAN member countries.

In South Asia in 2004, the SAARC proposed the establishment of a free-trade area (SAFTA) by 2006 and the lowering of tariff duties to 0–5 per cent in seven to ten years.

It is worth mentioning that the Shanghai Cooperation Organization, which connects China and five Central Asian countries, has also started to move into economic cooperation from its initial security and counter-terrorism cooperation. In September 2003, these countries signed an economic cooperation outline, setting out the three-stage development objectives of moving from facilitating trade and investment to the free flow of trade, services and investment by 2020. In July 2005, India, Pakistan and Iran were offered observer positions, bringing the organization one step closer toward accepting them as member countries.

In addition to the abovementioned, other subregional cooperation efforts in Asia include the Greater Mekong Subregion, Tumen River Area Development Programme, and Yellow Sea Rim Economic Region.

Asian regional integration still has a long way to go but such integration is following a generalized and continuous trend. Its significance is to offer a new path for regional cooperation. Furthermore, if it proves feasible, a new Asia with more than half the world's population, nearly a quarter of global GDP, and more than three-fifths the total foreign reserves of the world, will have a profound impact on the future shape of the world.

In the process of Asian integration, there is currently uneven development between East Asia and South Asia, with the former being the fastest-developing and the later lagging behind, relatively speaking. Nevertheless, India is now actively joining the East Asian integration process. India adopted the 'Looking East' policy in 1991. Along with the rapid growth of their economies, the economic connections between India and East Asia have increasingly expanded. India's overall trade in merchandise with East Asia more than doubled from about US$13 billion in 1997–98 to about US$27 billion in 2003–04, registering a compound annual growth rate of 13 per cent. In 2003–04, bilateral trade in merchandise between India and ASEAN accounted for 9.3 per cent of India's foreign trade, while that between India and ASEAN + 3 accounted for 19.9 per cent; the corresponding bilateral trade between India and the EU represented 19 per cent, while that with NAFTA accounted for 12.9 per cent (Ministry of Finance of India, 2005).

In order to further increase and facilitate trade between India and ASEAN, a Framework Agreement on establishing an FTA between ASEAN and India was signed in 2003, and negotiations have begun. The full implementation of the ASEAN–India FTA is expected by 2011 for the ASEAN-5 and by 2016 for Philippines and the CLMV countries. The participation of the India–ASEAN FTA will change ASEAN + 3 into ASEAN + 3 + 1 or JACIK (Japan, ASEAN, China, India and Korea).

History and status of economic relations between China and India

In the process of Asian regional integration, the development of Sino-Indian relations has attracted special attention around the world. China and India are two big neighbouring countries, separated by a long land border. They are symbolized by the dragon and the elephant. China is situated in the assembly centre of East Asia and now has a market with enormous demand, while India is the eminent regional power in South Asia. The development of Sino-Indian relations will not only have a great impact on the Asian integration process in connecting East Asia and South Asia but also, to a greater or lesser extent, on the emerging shape of the world. For the purpose of better understanding the direction of Sino-Indian relations and how far they could go, it is needed to look at the history and current status of economic relations between the two countries first.

Economic relations between China and India before the 1990s

Both China and India are great ancient countries and civilizations with a long history, and a centuries-old traditional friendship. The famous Eastern Jin Dynasty monk Faxian (334–420 AD) and the well-known Tang Dynasty monk Xuanzang (600–660 AD) left a legacy of many oft-told stories demonstrating the friendship between China and India. In the Ming Dynasty, Zheng He (1371–1435) sailed overseas seven times, bringing China and India into the closest contact of any period in their history. However, in the past few decades, due to the paths chosen for economic development and territorial disputes, economic exchanges between China and India were basically left at a standstill.

With regard to the respective paths they chose to develop their economies, China was isolated from the world economic system by the West after the start of the Cold War. Its own ideology also tended to seclude the country from the outside world. China developed through self-reliance and limited trade within the socialist camp's system. Meanwhile, having just gained independence from colonialism during the same period, India endeavoured to overtake the developed countries through a state-directed and import-substituting industrial development strategy. Although the respective starting points of the two countries to formulate economic policy were different, they ended with the same overall results. In their closed domestic markets, these two countries both set up relatively integrated industrial systems but, due to the overprotection of their respective domestic industries, they both had problems with inefficiency and a lack of international competitiveness. This development path meant that both China and India experienced slow development in overall foreign trade, not to mention trade between the two countries themselves. They could neither utilize international demand to promote domestic production and industrial upgrading nor had they any means to achieve the optimal allocation of resources and improve economic efficiency by participating in the international division of labour.

After China began to implement its reform and opening-up policies in 1978, accentuated differences in economic development began to emerge between China and India. Like other East Asian countries, China adopted an export-oriented path to develop its economy by actively participating in and exploiting the international division of labour, based on its competitive advantage of low-cost labour. During the two decades of reform, China has been aware of the need boldly to absorb and borrow ideas from the achievements of other civilizations, including those of the capitalist world, to narrow the gap between China and the developed countries. After 1992 when Deng Xiaoping made his famous speech during his inspection tour of South China, China's economic reform and opening-up entered a new era. Currently, China is the world's third-largest trading country. In 2004, its foreign trade was worth US$1,154.8 billion, of which exports were US$593.4 billion and imports US$561.4 billion. Foreign trade contributed to more than a quarter of economic growth and became an engine of economic growth. By the end of 2004, China had cumulatively attracted US$1,096.6 billion in foreign direct investment (FDI) and actually utilized US$562.1 billion. China has been ranked first among the developing countries for the utilization of FDI for 12 successive years. With foreign investment and trade promoting each other, China now plays an important role in the worldwide chain of production, and its rapidly growing domestic market is one of the engines of global economic growth. The Chinese economy is integrated into that of the wider world.

By contrast, the Indian economy was still in a relatively closed position until comparatively recent times. Even though India had implemented piecemeal privatization and opening-up measures in the 1980s, real systematic reform did not start until the 1990s.

These different development paths resulted in great differences emerging in the opening-up between these two countries. Measured from every angle, China is significantly more open than India. By 2005, China's average tariff rate had reached as low as 9 per cent, while this figure remained as high as 30 per cent in India. In 2004, China's total trade constituted 70 per cent of GDP, while India's trade was 30 per cent of its GDP. Furthermore, in 2004, China attracted US$60.6 billion in FDI, 9.4 per cent of the world's FDI inflow, while India attracted US$5.3 billion, 0.8 per cent of the world FDI inflow (United Nations Conference on Trade and Development, UNCTAD, 2005). During the period in which China rapidly developed its trade with the world, bilateral trade between China and India remained undeveloped.

The border disputes between China and India also cast a negative shadow on the development of economic relations between the two countries. For historical reasons, there has been no officially defined border between China and India, giving rise to territorial disputes over a large area. In 1962, an unpleasant border war broke out between the two countries, which restricted the development of Sino-Indian relations to a large extent and made these two countries keep a watchful eye on each other even long after the war itself, given that the border issue is related to each country's fundamental interests and national sentiments.

For the aforementioned reasons, China and India have had highly limited economic exchanges for a long time. Official trade between China and India started in 1951, and the governments of the two countries signed a trade agreement in October 1954. However, for decades the scale of bilateral trade was very small and developed slowly. From 1950 to 1962 bilateral trade was worth only US$260 million, and then due to the border war was interrupted for 14 years until 1976, when China and India resumed diplomatic relations and bilateral trade was restored. In August 1984 the two governments signed a new trade agreement, and since 1986 seven annual trade agreements have been signed. By the 1990s, China and India had opened several entrepôts in border regions, including the restored trade between Plan in China's Tibet Autonomous Region and Gunji in the India state of Uttar Pradesh in 1992, and the newly opened trade between Jiuba in China's Tibet and Nangal in the Indian state of Himachal Pradesh in 1994. On the whole, trade between China and India was rather small before the 1990s and remained so even during the early 1990s.

Economic relations between China and India since the 1990s

The rapid development of India's economy and trade has brought Sino-Indian economic relations to a new phase. A decade after China's opening-up, India also started its systematic economic reform, embracing deregulation, marketization and globalization. During the past decade, its average annual GDP growth reached 6.5 per cent, its trade openness increased from 15 per cent to 30 per cent, and tariff and non-tariff barriers dropped from 128 per cent to 30 per cent. In 2004, India's foreign trade amounted to US$188.1 billion. Of this, exports were worth US$79.8 billion, up 24.4 per cent from the year before; and imports were worth US$108.2 billion, up 35.6 per cent. In August 2004, India announced its *National Foreign Trade Policy 2004–2009* (Department of Commerce of India, 2004) and laid down the ambitious target of achieving an export growth rate that would enable India to account for 1.5 per cent of world trade by 2009. Furthermore, India also actively adopted measures to attract FDI, and has now become one of the most popular investment destinations along with the United States and China. Foreign investment mainly focuses on such sectors as power, which occupies 26.8 per cent of total FDI; pharmaceuticals, 10.6 per cent; and consultancy services, 8.0 per cent. Usually the most competitive sectors are also those that draw the most investment, and such investment activities could further increase India's export capabilities and external competitiveness.

Sino-Indian economic relations have been accelerating since the end of the 1990s, as represented in trade, investment, technological cooperation and other exchanges and communications, as well as in other areas.

From 1999 to 2004, bilateral trade increased from US$1.99 billion to US$13.6 billion (Figure 3.1). China's exports to India grew from US$1.16 billion to US$5.93 billion, and imports grew from US$830 million to US$7.68 billion. The robust growth continued in 2005 when, from January to July, trade between the two countries reached US$10.76 billion, a year-on-year rise of 39.8 per cent. Of this trade, China's exports to India were worth US$4.67 billion, a year-on-year increase of 58.8 per cent, and imports from India were worth US$6.09 billion, a year-on-year rise of 28.1 per cent (Ministry of Commerce, China, 2005). Bilateral trade focuses on natural resources and energy, electrical machinery, pharmaceuticals, organic chemicals, IT products, and so on; India mainly imported electrical machinery, organic chemicals and silk from China, while China mainly imported iron ore, steel, plastics and organic chemical products from India.

Sino-Indian investment is also thriving. Indian companies come to China not only because of the market's huge potential but also for the infrastructure facilities and preferential policies and regulations which make Indian companies competitive worldwide. The main reason for Chinese enterprises investing in India is to avoid India's high trade barriers.

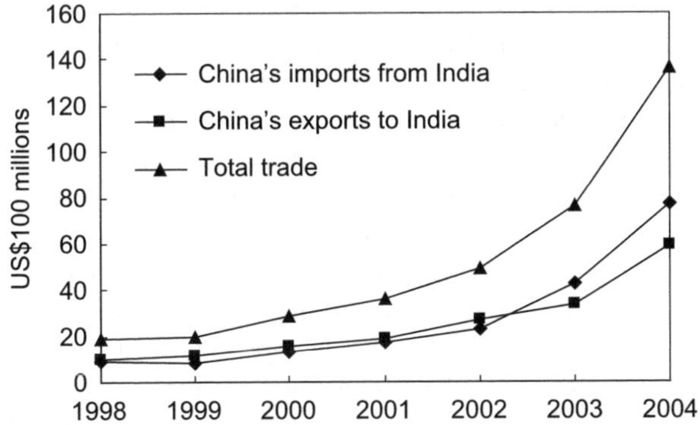

Figure 3.1 Trade-development between China and India, 1998–2004
Source: MOFCOM (Ministry of Commerce of China), China.

By April 2005, India had signed up to US$235 million worth of FDI agreements in China (*India Today*, 2005). The investment is mainly in high-tech and knowledge-intensive industries such as software, pharmaceuticals and the biotechnology industries, and in car parts and low-added-value manufacturing industries such as diamond processing, the production of fireproof and packaging materials, and so on. In terms of diamond enterprises alone, 19 enterprises have entered China, scattered over several areas such as Shanghai, Shandong, Guangzhou, and others.

By the end of 2004, China had invested US$22.8 million an aggregate in India, focused mainly on IT, natural resources and white goods.

In addition to trade and investment, the relations between the two countries have also advanced comprehensively in services, tourism, scientific and technological cooperation, the movement of labour and border negotiations, for example. With regard to services, there is a lack of accurate data, but some examples can give a general idea of their status. At present, four major Indian software enterprises – Tata Consultancy Services, Infosys Technologies, Wipro Technologies, and Satyam Computer Services – have all invested in China. Of these, Infosys Technologies has established a software development centre in China. In 2005, Tata Consultancy Services was selected as an IT partner by the China National Development and Reform Commission to offer IT-related services. And the long-term Chinese IT training market has basically been monopolized by two Indian–Chinese joint venture companies, namely the NIIT (National Institute of Information Technology of India) Information Technology School and Aptech Beida Jade Bird Information Technology Co Ltd. Concerning tourism, the India–China Tourism Agreement signed in 2002 opened the door to tourism between the two countries. The two countries are preparing to open new flight routes and increase the number of flights to each other's country. In the field of scientific and technological cooperation, India's technology for the peaceful use of atomic energy, agriculture, genetic engineering, personal computer (PC) technologies, and particularly software development, are of interest for China. China's small-scale blast furnace, mini-hydropower, household appliance, space development and other technologies also have interested India. The two countries have already signed cooperation agreements and/or memoranda of cooperation and understanding in most of these fields, and positive results have been achieved. Several joint ventures involving large amounts of investment have been put into operation, and the governments and business communities are further exploring ways and approaches to cooperate further. In addition, the two countries also signed cooperation memoranda for personnel exchanges and labour cooperation. Regarding the border dispute, the premiers of the two countries appointed special representatives in June 2003 to explore ways to solve the border problem, and through five rounds of contacts the two countries have reached a consensus on guidelines for solving the problems. The sixth round of negotiations, held in September 2005, brought the negotiations to a substantial phase.

With the premiers of the two countries exchanging visits in 2003 and 2005, Sino–Indian relations have been comprehensively upgraded, symbolizing that China and India have entered a new phase of cooperation.

The rise of both China and India will be one of the significant themes and phenomena of the twenty-first century. As Asian economic integration deepens and the economies of both countries develop rapidly, new conditions are being created for reshaping Sino-Indian relations. In addition, discussion of Sino-Indian relations has been put on the global agenda. Looking ahead, the cooperation and strengthened economic relations between the two countries mean a lot of common benefits for both countries. However, there are also a series of impediments to further cooperation.

Incentives for Sino-Indian cooperation

China and India have greater and greater mutual interests and mutual gains that can be realized through Sino-Indian cooperation include the following:

- Firstly, broader gains from trade shall be obtained through enlargement of the scope and scale of their common markets. Although bilateral trade and investment are rapidly developing, they are presently insignificant considering the economic scale of the two countries (Figure 3.2). In 2004, foreign trade with India accounted for just 1.2 per cent of China's total foreign trade, of which exports accounted for 1.0 per cent of China's total exports, and imports accounted for 1.4 per cent of total imports (Ministry of Commerce, China, 2005). According to statistics from India (Department of

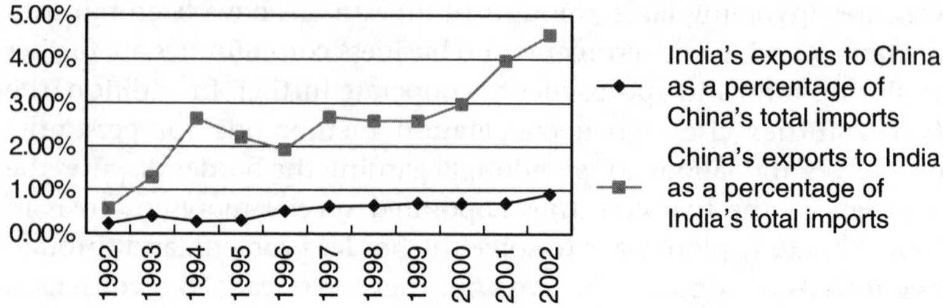

Figure 3.2 India's and China's exports in proportion to the other's imports
Source: Calculated from the UN COMTRADE database.

Commerce, India, 2005), its foreign trade with China in 2004 accounted for just 5 per cent of its overall foreign trade, of which exports accounted for 4.6 per cent and imports accounted for 5.2 per cent. FDI is also very small between China and India. China's investment in India is less than 1 per cent of its overall foreign investment. Although India had a slightly higher investment percentage in China over the last two years, amounting to between 3 per cent and 6 per cent, India's foreign investment scale is fundamentally smaller than that of China. In 2004, India's total foreign investment stock was just one-fifth that of China.

- There is thus a lot of room for China and India to enlarge the scale of their bilateral trade. They are the two largest developing countries in the world, India having a population of 1.07 billion, and China having a population of more than 1.3 billion. Added together, they account for one-third of the total world population, and 6 per cent of the world's total GDP. Moreover, they have also been enjoying the fastest economic growth among the world's larger economies. From 1980 to 2004, China's average annual GDP reached 9.2 per cent, while since the beginning of economic reform in the 1990s India's annual growth rate has reached 6.5 per cent and, in recent years, growth figures even reached 7 per cent to 8 per cent. Although both countries' GDP per capita is still low, the potential scale of the market in the two countries is huge, based on their large populations and GDP and their sustained rates of economic growth, especially when world markets are otherwise becoming saturated in developed countries. China's and India's opening of their respective domestic markets to each other will bring an exponential increase in trade and investment opportunities, thus enhancing the tremendous gains from trade for both countries.

- Secondly, rapid economic development may be derived from deepening the international division of labour. Although the level of economic development is still low in both countries, the economic structures of China and India complement each other to a relatively strong degree. The reasons for this lie in the fact that both countries have their own absolute or relative advantages in various factors and products, and that economic reform and opening-up was initiated earlier and more broadly in China than in India.
- According to the World Bank (2005), agriculture had a 15 per cent share of China's GDP, industry 52 per cent, and services 33 per cent in 2003, while agriculture accounted for 22 per cent of India's GDP, industry 27 per cent and services 51 per cent.
- Compared with India, China is more competitive in manufacturing, with a better-trained and low-cost workforce. Its manufacturing sector accounts for 39 per cent of China's GDP and is mainly aimed at exports, making China known as a world assembly centre, the 'workshop of the world'. As well as conventional labour-intensive consumer goods, China's competitiveness has become increasingly stronger in electrical and electronic products assembly in recent years. In contrast, India's productivity in the manufacturing industry is lower than that in China. The estimates of Gopalan (2001) in relation to labour productivity in manufacturing suggest that, except for petroleum products and non-electrical machinery, the productivity of a Chinese worker is higher than that of an Indian worker by anywhere from 30 per cent to 180 per cent, depending on the product.
- India's competitiveness is primarily reflected in high-tech industries, including software and IT services, and India regards the software industry as a key part of its national development strategy. Through increased investment in higher education and tax preferences, the software industry is growing at an annual rate of more than 26 per cent. In 2003, the exports of the software industry were worth US$9.5 billion, accounting for 20 per cent of India's overall exports. Now, India's share of world service exports has reached 1.5 per cent. Of this, the great majority comprises information technology and related services. Due to its competitiveness in IT

services, India is becoming the 'back-office of the world' serving more and more European and US enterprises.

- In addition to information technology, India has also shown competitive advantages in pharmaceuticals, biotechnology and some other high-tech products. Indian Chamber of Commerce and Industry (ICCI) research shows that the productivity of India's pharmaceutical industry has grown by 10 per cent annually during the past decade, compared with 7 per cent for the world as a whole. Today, the scale of India's pharmaceutical industry ranks fourth in the world, and its pharmaceutical output ranks 13th. By 2007, the production potential of India's pharmaceutical industry is expected to reach US$48 billion (*India Today*, 2005).
- In contrast, China's service sector, especially the software and IT services, lags behind, relatively speaking. In 2003, commercial services comprised 10.6 per cent of total trade in China, while the figure for India was 26.9 per cent. Furthermore, the technological content of services is low in China. Financial and insurance services, and other commercial services, including computer, information and communications services, comprise 45.4 per cent of total commercial services in China, while the figure is 76.6 per cent in India (calculated from WB, 2005).
- China's advantages in industrial and mechanical equipment and processing, and India's advantages in software and the high-tech industry, create complementary spaces for the two countries to cooperate in vertical and horizontal specialization.
- Vertical specialization has already emerged in these two countries and is continually deepening and expanding. From 1999 to 2002, primary products as a proportion of China's total exports to India decreased from 33.1 per cent to 19.5 per cent. In the corresponding period, manufactured products increased from 66.9 per cent to 80.5 per cent, of which machinery and transport equipment exports accounted for 35 per cent of manufactured product exports. In recent years, with high economic growth, China's imports have expanded rapidly. Indian exporters find ever-increasing opportunities in China's intermediate input market, and exports of dye, primary plastics, steel and other metals, and pulp have increased rapidly.
- Horizontal specialization has also been growing rapidly, which is highlighted in two major fields: motor vehicles, and PC software and hardware.

- Indian motor vehicle manufacturers have entered the Chinese market in a timely manner in recent years. To date, bilateral trade under this heading has not been large but it is growing rapidly. In 2002, Chinese imports from India were worth US$6.0 million and exports to India were worth US$4.0 million. From January to July 2003, imports from India increased by 355% and exports rose by 50.5 per cent. Regarding PC technology, China's hardware processing industry and India's software and service industries show strong potential for cooperation. The then premier of India, Atal Bihari Vajpayee, said on his visit to China in 2003 that China's [hardware] products and India's [software] solution complemented each other, constituting the natural foundation for sustained cooperation between the two countries. He said that both Chinese and Indian enterprises should cooperate directly.
- Thirdly, enhanced bargaining strength in the process of formulating international rules shall be enabled, so as to protect and promote the two countries' common interests as developing major powers.
- Despite the increasing power of both China and India, each of them individually has no effective means to counterbalance today's global system. Kenneth Waltz defined 'power' as the 'extent that [one] affects others more than they affect [oneself]'. A state's power can thus be understood as a combination of that state's capacity to influence others to behave as it wants them to behave and, conversely, to resist the unwelcome influences of others. Based on this definition, Perkovich (2003) argued that:

  > India today lacks great power in that, for the most part, it cannot make other important states comply with Indian demands, nor can it obtain all that it desires in the international arena, although India does have the capacity to resist most if not all demands placed upon it by other states, including the recognized major powers.

- As far as China is concerned, China can influence other countries' behaviour in some respects and can resist the demands made by other countries but, in comparison, the impact of other countries on China is larger than China's impact on other countries.
- The current international economic system is still dominated by the Western developed countries, particularly the United States. This is reflected in the financial and trade institutions based on the

post-Bretton Woods system and WTO. As two rising developing great powers, China and India potentially challenge the interests that the Western countries have traditionally enjoyed, and hence face strong resistance from the West. With regard to trade, the protectionism from Western countries has been surging as they deal with the rapid development of both China and India. China faces a strong degree of protectionism against its increased manufacturing exports, while the outsourcing of services to India is also generating opposition from Western countries, even though this protectionism is inconsistent with the free-trade principles of the WTO. In respect of finance and exchange rates, China has accumulated large foreign reserves, US$609.9 billion in 2004. Although it enjoys a large trade surplus with the United States, overall trade basically is balanced. China has been accused of having an undervalued exchange rate. Like China, India also has an increasing foreign-reserve surplus, US$141.2 billion in 2004. Outsourcing is likely to bring a greater surplus to its current-account balance. India's exchange regime has been a managed floating one, and China too adopted a more flexible exchange-rate regime in July 2005. Since then, the RMB exchange rate has increased. But this is far less than what is demanded by the United States. Currently both China and India have not liberalized their capital accounts, and there remain substantial capital controls. With the US trade deficit accumulating and unemployment increasing, both countries are likely to be criticized of exchange-rate manipulation.

- Against this background, China and India have more and more mutual interests and, on many issues, their claims and requirements based on their differing social conditions are unlike from those of the West. Through Sino-Indian cooperation, the two countries' bargaining strength can be increased in the process of formulating future international rules to guarantee their interests and win favourable 'rules of the game' for developing countries, including themselves. China and India have cooperated in the WTO and G20 organizations. For example, India, in cooperation with Brazil and China, played a key role in developing a consensus at the WTO General Council meeting in Geneva in July 2004. Such cooperation is likely to expand in the future.
- Fourthly, higher costs can be avoided in the exploration and exploitation of natural resources and energy. Both China and India

are experiencing three similar economic reforms and social shifts: from a planned or heavily regulated economy to a market economy; from an agricultural economy to a modern economy; and from a closed economy to one that is opening up. A significant challenge to the world can be foreseen as the two countries follow the Western mode of development at the same time. Currently, the two countries have faced similar resource constraints in their economic development and both have an increasing demand for resources such as copper, iron ore and petroleum, which is viewed as challenge to the world supply of energy and natural resources.

- Now, one-third of China's and two-thirds of India's oil consumption depends on imports. In *Mapping the Global Future* (National Intelligence Council, 2004), the US National Intelligence Council (NIC) indicates that China will need to boost its energy consumption by about 150 per cent and India will need to nearly double its consumption by 2020 to maintain a steady rate of economic growth. This report anticipates that 'the energy needs will be the major factor in shaping China and India's foreign and defense policies including expanding their naval power'.
- If the two countries compete with each other for energy exploration in the world market, the result will be disadvantageous to them both and even the world, and fierce competition in the worst-case scenario could even result in war. History teaches that mutual benefits can be achieved by establishing an institutionalized process of cooperation. Taking account of each other's interests, the two countries can coordinate with each other to explore new energy sources and to undertake technological cooperation for the efficient utilization of energy and natural resources.
- Fifthly, border security can be created, laying a favourable foundation for mutual economic development.
- China and India are undergoing unprecedented domestic development and reform, and both very much need peaceful external environments to succeed in their economic reform policies. China is a neighbour of 20 countries, of which India is very significant to the security of China's southwestern border. Similarly, India has been alert to its northeastern neighbour for a long time. Historically these two countries built up rancour and lack mutual trust. However, as noted earlier, economic integration contributes to bringing about peace, and thus the development of Sino-Indian trade relations

helps create a foundation for peaceful external security for both countries. It is noteworthy that, since 2003, India's Department of Defence has excluded China from the list of threats to India in its annual report, and military communications between the two countries have begun. Security relations between the two countries are being reshaped and restructured constructively.

Impediments to Sino-Indian relations

Although Sino-Indian cooperation promises vast mutual benefits for both China and India, some political and economic factors continue to create bottlenecks and obstacles in the development of Sino-Indian relations.

First of all, conflicts of interest are inherent among domestic interest groups in both countries. China's political system gave the government the authority to implement its opening-up policies once China decided to do so, and unless exceptional social instability is encountered such a path is unlikely to be reversed. But it cannot be denied that, as relevant political and economic structures change, interest groups are playing increasingly obvious roles in China and exerting an ever-greater influence in the formulation of economic policies. Kennedy (2005) comprehensively surveyed industries including steel, electronic products and software in China and found that lobbying was becoming popular in China. The interest groups lobby government officials by telephone, email and personal visits, and they can have an increasingly significant effect on taxation, technical standards and intellectual property policies. In the formulation of China's exchange-rate policy, some research shows that export departments, particularly of state-owned enterprises connected to local governments, have exercised outstanding influence in the lobbying of government, which induces policies to veer in directions that benefit these export departments (Zhang Yuyan and Zhang Jingchun, 2005). China's interest groups are developing increasingly, and they will surely exert an increasing influence in the development of Sino-Indian relations.

India's much more diversified interest groups and democratic politics mean that India faces even greater resistance to economic reform and free trade compared to China. India is now implementing a system of representative democracy, and it features a diversified, multi-religion and multi-level social structure. For a long time, India maintained a balance between its multifarious groups, and even British colonialism failed to break this. Singh (1999) said that from the point of view of civilization, India is a diversified entity; compared with China, India has existed in a somewhat stateless condition while China has always existed in a unified and hierarchical condition. India's central and local governments, as well as all kinds of interest groups, are highly decentralized and they often compete with each other.

This social and political system makes it difficult for India to mobilize its social forces as a whole to move in any decisive direction. Although the national interest is felt to be supreme, domestic conflicts of interest make it hard to implement a unified policy. Although most parties use opening-up and free trade as campaign slogans and profess intense political will, it is very difficult in reality to move free trade forward. For instance, although there are calls for the reduction of agricultural subsidies, reform has seldom really touched these fields due to opposition from vested interest groups and the lack of effective political will. Another example is that, although the service sector calls for freer trade, small and medium-sized enterprises, family businesses and their allied forces also hamper progress towards further reform. When it comes to opening-up in India, the free-trade measures that are implemented relate mainly to the promotion of exports and the introduction of FDI. Progress toward liberalizing the domestic market, however, remains limited.

Considering that China's competitive manufacturing industry may harm some vested interests in India, protective measures and resistance from India make the development of Sino-Indian relations potentially difficult.

Secondly, geopolitical considerations and the coexistence of economic cooperation and competition in the two countries are important factors. Both China and India are highly conscious of the prospect of becoming prosperous and wealthy countries, and hope to re-establish themselves among the world's major powers in terms of industry, technology, trade and finance through economic development. Similar approaches adopted to achieve such objectives determine that these two countries are inevitably in competition with each other.

Although India is highly competitive in IT and related services, taken as a whole this sector accounts for only around 3 per cent of the entire GDP and employs around 1 million people. The history of successfully industrialized economies suggests that modernization cannot be achieved without a developed manufacturing sector. Unexceptionally, India's economic development cannot bypass the industrialization stage, especially considering that industrialization is an indispensable step for providing employment opportunities and reducing the number of people suffering from poverty.[7] Owing to the irreplaceable role played by the manufacturing sector in the industrialization process and the unwillingness of India to watch its manufacturing sector wither as a result of competition from China, India has tried to take measures in the hope of protecting and stimulating the sector.

On 26 September 2005, India's National Manufacturing Competitiveness Committee (NMCC) published a draft of the *National Strategy for Manufacturing* (NMCC, 2005), proposing a 12 per cent annual growth rate for India's manufacturing industry in the coming decades. This growth rate is regarded as a guarantee for India's overall economic growth rate of 9 per cent. The report also pointed out that India would compete with China for the position of the world's assembly or manufacturing centre by creating more favourable policy environment. In 2005 the Global Economic Forum (GEF) issued the *2005–2006 Global Competitiveness Report* (GEF, 2005), indicating that the competitiveness of China and India ranked 49th and 50th respectively, with China dropping three places and India rising five.

In this context, China's products and enterprises have made little progress in the Indian market despite their global competitiveness. One main reason is that Indian governments erect trade and non-trade barriers against China's products and enterprises. By September 2005, India had initiated 85 cases of anti-dumping investigations against China, and the number of cases being implemented even outnumbered those taken by the United States, which makes India the country that has raised the most anti-dumping cases against China (WTO, 2005a). In a few months in 2005, India raised seven anti-dumping investigations against China, involving about US$250 million. Of these cases, the anti-dumping investigation of 18 May 2005 relating to imported Chinese silk fabric involved US$180 million, the highest amount in a single anti-dumping investigation raised by India against China in the past few years.

India's Foreign Investment Promotion Committee has occasionally suspended the review of investment projects from China for reasons of 'national security', and such reviews have even included durable goods.

According to *The Times of India* of 16 August 2005, the Indian government had twice used such an approach in the past five years to postpone the expansion of the Chinese firm Huawei Technologies in India. The newspaper described the government's behaviour towards Huawei Technologies as 'a hard decision between cheap Chinese products and India's national security'.

In the case of China, in order to ensure sustainable economic growth, policy-makers have to find a proper way to complete the process of industrialization and urbanization. At present, China faces two somewhat competing targets: upgrading its industrial structure and creating numerous job opportunities simultaneously. The sustainable development will remain a dream if China does not catch up with the industrialized economies in terms of technology-intensive products and cope successfully with the politically sensitive problem of employment. This situation requires China to continue its opening-up strategy on the one hand – that is absorbing FDI and actively participating in global production at the low end, and providing more job opportunities to the domestic workforce – and boosting its own high-tech and high-value-added and environmentally friendly industries on the other hand. All of this indicates that India's strongly regulated and limited market cannot satisfy the needs of both Chinese exports and investment. Recently, China has revealed its determination to support the development of the software sector. This means, more or less, that Indian competitiveness in software and outsourcing may be challenged by Chinese competition.

Thirdly, the economic development of both China and India depends a great deal on external markets, especially the US market. However, due to considerations of its own national interests, the United States does not and will not support the building of closer alliance-like relations between China and India.

Currently, the economic development of both China and India relies very much on the United States, the superpower of today's world, to provide the required market, capital, technology, and so on. At the same time, US dependence on these two countries is much less. To a great extent, such disproportionate interdependence determines that the United States has much greater leverage in bilateral relations with either of the two countries.

It can be seen in *America's National Interests* (Commission on America's National Interests, 2000) that one of the vital interests of the United States is to maintain its leadership worldwide and deter the emergence of a hostile major power in its neighbouring regions. In *Mapping the Global Future*, the National Intelligence Committee pointed out that, in the next 15 years, China and India would become global powers. This report predicted that China's GDP would be the second biggest in the world by 2020, next only to that of the United States. By then, India would outdo most European countries, and both China and India might become world technological leaders.

Were China and India to form an alliance, they would pose a credible challenge to the United States. For the benefit of its national interests, the United States prevents China and India from developing an even closer strategic alliance through the United States itself developing closer relations with India. The United States changed its Cold War mentality towards India and described US–Indian relations as an even closer new partnership. Bill Clinton's visit to India in 2000 signalled that US–Indian relations had entered a new era, and since the Bush administration took the reins of power, US–Indian relations have warmed continually. In order to highlight how the United States and India are different from China and to weaken the common sense of identity between China and India, the United States defined US–Indian relations as 'cooperation between the two largest democracies'. In March 2005, the Bush administration promulgated a project, with a view to enhancing the strategic communication with India and deepening bilateral cooperation in high-tech, economic and energy areas. The United States claimed that it would help India to become a great power for the twenty-first century. In April 2005, President George W. Bush held talks with India's Minister of Foreign Affairs, Natwar Singh, and said that US–Indian relations would be elevated to a 'higher level'.

One of the main purposes for developing US–Indian relations is to target the rise of China. In a report, Tellis (2005) pointed out that, thanks to the tremendous development potential of India in the next 20 to 25 years, the Bush administration should help India grow into an Asian superpower to counterbalance China. This report suggested that the United States ought to adopt five measures to build up an alliance with India, which are: helping India to develop in order to prevent China from growing into the leading power in Asia; abandoning the illusion of keeping a military balance between India and Pakistan; supporting India's request for permanent membership of the United Nations Security Council and helping India to join the

Group of Eight (G8), the Asia-Pacific Economic Cooperation forum (APEC) and the International Atomic Energy Agency (IAEA); agreeing to construct an Iran-Pakistan-India oil and gas pipeline; and selling dual-purpose nuclear engineering technology including nuclear safety equipment to India, and so on.

Some people think that the US-led Western world deliberately compares China and India with a geopolitical strategic intention. By highlighting the competing features between these two countries, the consensus between China and India will be weakened, thus preventing them from forming a strategic alliance.

Prospects of Sino-Indian relations

Since the late 1980s, the changing shape of the world, the deepening of Asian economic integration, and the rapid economic development of China and India have created the necessary conditions for the reshaping of Sino-Indian relations. China and India have already ended their long history of self-imposed isolation. Cooperation means a wide range of mutual benefits for both countries, such as realizing and expanding trade gains, promoting economic growth, enhancing bargaining strength in the process of formulating international rules, avoiding higher costs in exploring natural resources and energy, as well as maintaining a peaceful border, something that is conducive and indispensable to economic development. Meanwhile, a series of factors – conflicts of interest among domestic groups in the two countries, economic competition and geopolitical considerations between China and India, and the pressure or influence of external powers – restricts the depth and extent to which the two countries can cooperate further.

There are three scenarios for Sino-Indian relations. The first scenario is that China and India will remain isolated from each other, and that a zero-sum competitive relationship will exist between China and India. At the same time, the two countries will inevitably compete with each other as they grow stronger. Realistically, it is hardly possible to return to the situation in which the two countries found themselves before. The second scenario is the establishment of a full-fledged bilateral free-trade area and the formation of an overall strategic alliance between the two countries in the global arena. However, the incentives and impediments that lie ahead of Sino-Indian economic relations determine that this is also unlikely to happen, at least in the short term. The third scenario is that Sino-Indian cooperation will move slowly and smoothly toward mutual prosperity but the relationship between the two countries will generally develop on a 'being good neighbours' basis. Based on the above analysis, this scenario may actually be the most likely relationship between China and India.

The term 'being good neighbours' needs to be elaborated in a little more detail. Such a relationship between China and India has four aspects: the maintenance of long-term peaceful coexistence; the keeping of political and economic differences and conflicts manageable; the further opening of markets and the facilitating of economic cooperation in fields of mutual benefit; and strengthened cooperation on specific issues at regional and international levels. Good fences make good neighbours. Here, 'good fences' refers to clearly defined and strictly enforced international rules or institutions. In the case of Sino-Indian relations, the two countries can intensify communication and cooperation within the framework of JACIK and the Shanghai Cooperation Organization, and they can also cooperate within the framework of the WTO and G20. The cooperation between them, albeit gradually strengthened and specific-areas focused, will contribute to Asian economic integration, to the common interest of developing countries, and the welfare of the human being as a whole.

Notes

1 Here transaction costs refer to all kinds of non-production costs. For further discussion of transaction costs, see Coase (1937).

2 Substantial empirical evidence exists to support the proposition that economic integration reduces conflicts between nations. See, for instance, Polacheck (1980). By utilizing data from 30 countries in the 1958–67 period, Polacheck showed that a doubling of trade between two countries led to a 20% decline in the frequency of hostilities.

3 This is similar to Ronald Coase's Theory of the Firm. The boundary of economic integration is dependent on the contrast between the reduced transaction costs generated from the internalization of transactions and the increased costs in scaling-up as a result. See Coase (1937).

4 Asia here specifically refers to the East Asian countries of China, Japan and South Korea; the ASEAN/AFTA 10 countries of Brunei Darussalam, Cambodia, Indonesia, Laos, Malaysia, Myanmar, the Philippines, Singapore, Thailand and Vietnam; the South Asian Association for Regional Cooperation (SAARC) countries of Bangladesh, Bhutan, India, the Maldives, Nepal, Pakistan and Sri Lanka; and the Shanghai Cooperation Organization member countries of China, Kazakhstan, Kyrgyzstan, Tajikistan, Uzbekistan, and the Asian parts of Russia.

5 For detailed discussion of the 'flying-geese' model, see Kojima (2000).

6 Share of trade alone does not provide a sufficient indication of the extent to which the home country regards its trading partners as being important in relation to that country's trade with the rest of the world. For this reason, the trade intensity index is considered a more useful tool for measuring bilateral trade. It is calculated as $[Xii/\{(Xiw + Xwi)/2\}]/[\{(Xiw + Xwi)/2\}/Xww]$ where Xww is total world exports. An index rating that is greater (or less) than one unit indicates that the trade flow is larger (or smaller) than would be expected, given the region's importance in world trade – i.e., the index takes account of the region's relative size in world trade and provides a more accurate measure of trade integration within a region. See Kawai (2005).

7 According to the World Bank's *World Development Indicators 2005*, the number of people living in poverty in India is estimated at 260 million to 290 million. If measured by the international living standard of those living on less than US$1 per day, the figure would be 390 million.

References

Coase, R. (1937) 'The Nature of the Firm', *Economica*, vol. 4, pp. 386–405.

Commission on America's National Interests (2000) *America's National Interests*. Washington, DC: The Commission on America's National Interests.

Department of Commerce of India (2004) *National Foreign Trade Policy 2004–2009*. New Delhi: Department of Commerce.

— (2005) http://commerce.nic.in/india_trade.htm. New Delhi: Department of Commerce.

Global Economic Forum (2005) *2005–2006 Global Competitiveness Report*. Davos: Global Economic Forum.

Gopalan, R. (2001) 'China's Competitiveness', Discussion Paper. New Delhi: Department of Commerce, Government of India (mimeo).

India Today (2005) 'Indian Economic News', April 2005, p. 16.

Kawai, M. (2005) 'Trade and Investment Integration for Development in East Asia: A Case for the Trade–FDI Nexus'. Washington, DC: World Bank, ABCDE Europe Meeting.

Kennedy, S. (2005) *The Business of Lobbying in China*. Cambridge, Mass.: Harvard University Press.

Kojima, K. (2000) 'The "Flying Geese" Model of Asian Economic Development: Origin, Theoretical Extensions, and Regional Policy Implications', *Journal of Asian Economics*, vol. 11, issue 4, Autumn, pp. 375–401.

Ministry of Commerce of China (2005) http://www.mofcom.gov.cn. MOFCOM.

Ministry of Finance of India (2005) http://indiabudget.nic.in/es2004–05/chapt2005/chap66.pdf. Ministry of India.

National Intelligence Committee (2004) *Mapping the Global Future: Report of the National Intelligence Council's 2020 Project, Based on Consultations With Nongovernmental Experts Around the World*. Washington, DC: National Intelligence Committee.

National Manufacturing Competitiveness Committee (2005) *National Strategy for Manufacturing*. New Delhi: National Manufacturing Competitiveness Committee.

Olson, M. (1965) *The Logic of Collective Action: Public Goods and the Theory of Groups*. Cambridge: Harvard University Press.

Perkovich, G. (2004) 'Is India a Major Power?' *The Washington Quarterly*, Volume 27, Number 1, Winter 2003–04, pp. 129–144. The MIT Press.

Polacheck, S. (1980) 'Conflict and Trade' *Journal of Conflict Resolution* 24 (April).

Rajan, R. S. and Sen, R. (2004) 'Asian Economic Cooperation and Integration: Sequencing of Financial, Trade and Monetary Regionalism,' ADB Volume on Asian Economic Cooperation and Integration.

Singh, J. (1999) *Defending India*. London and New Delhi: Macmillan.

Tellis, Ashley, J. (2005) 'India as a Global Power: An Action Agenda for the United States,' Washington DC: Carnegie Endowment for International Peace.

The Times of India, 16 August 2005.

UNCTAD (2005) *World Investment Report 2005*, UNCTAD: Geneva.

World Bank (2005) *World Development Indicators 2005*, Washington, DC: The World Bank.

WTO (2005a) http://www.wto.org/english/tratop_e/adp_e/adp_e.htm#statistics.

WTO (2005b) http://www.wto.org/english/tratop_e/region_e/region_e.htm.

Zhang Yuyan (1992) *Economic Development and the Choice of Institutions*, Renming University Press.

Zhang Yuyan and Zhang Jingchun (2005) 'The International Political Economy of Exchange Rates: A Case Study of the RMB based on the Debate Between China and the US,' *Contemporary Asian-Pacific Studies*, No. 9.

4
Economic Cooperation between Thailand and India and its Implications for the Asian Community*

Chularat Suteethorn

Background

Globalization has made countries more interconnected in every aspect, especially in their economic activities. After the 2003 WTO ministerial meetings in Cancún failed to yield results, many countries have chosen to negotiate bilateral or regional trade arrangements on their own as an alternative route to speed up trade liberalization.

Thailand has been negotiating Free Trade Area Agreements with its strategic trading partners to expand and diversify its export markets. Many of these have already been implemented, such as ASEAN and China Free Trade Area (FTA), Thailand and Australia FTA, Thailand and New Zealand FTA, and Thailand and India FTA (only products in Early Harvest Scheme). Moreover, many are being finalized such as Thailand and Japan as part of the ASEAN–Japan FTA, and some are under negotiation, for instance Thailand and the US FTA, Thailand and Peru FTA, Bay of Bengal Initiative for Multi-Sectoral Technical and Economic-Cooperation (BIMSTEC) FTA, Thailand and Bahrain FTA and so on.

India is also a major player in this trend. India has been negotiating several Free Trade Areas such as the South Asia Free Trade Area (SAFTA),

---

* This chapter expresses the view of author and does not necessarily represent the view of the Fiscal Policy Office. The author would like to thank Ruecha Varatorn and Elcid Vergara for preparing data and necessary information and help in editing this chapter.

ASEAN and India Free Trade Area, India and Singapore Free Trade Area, India and Sri Lanka Free Trade Area, India and Bhutan Free Trade Area and India and Nepal Free Trade Area. Such developments are being felt throughout Asia.

India and Thailand have enjoyed a long relationship, stretching back many centuries, that can be seen in culture, tradition, language and social similarities. In the trade aspect, Thailand and India have established formal trade cooperation since 1968, and the Joint Trade Committee was signed in 1985 to further accelerate collaboration. Several key agreements followed to facilitate investors on both sides, such as the double taxation agreement in 1985, the trade and investment promotion agreement in 1997, and the investment enhancement and protection agreement in 2000.

In addition, as a member of both ASEAN and BIMSTEC, Thailand plays a pivotal role in linking India to ASEAN and East Asian Countries (China, Japan and Korea). Thailand and India have signed several bilateral and regional Free Trade Area agreements as follows: the Framework Agreement on Comprehensive Economic Co-operation between the Association of South-East Asian Nations and the Republic of India in 2003, the Framework Agreement for Establishing a Free Trade Area between Thailand and India in 2003, and the Framework Agreement on the BIMSTEC Free Trade Area in 2004.

Both Thai and India private sectors recognize the importance of their trade relationship and they have also signed several agreements and established councils or committees in order to foster their trade and investment. The agreements are as follows: the Agreement on cooperation between the Thai Industrial Council and the India Chamber of Commerce and Industry in 1990, and the Thai–India Trade Council that was founded in the same year. In 2004, the Thai–South Asia Business Forum was set up to discuss issues regarding trade barriers between the Thai private sector/government and South Asia countries' governments, including India.

Thai–Indian economic relationships

Trade in goods

Although diplomatic relationships have subsisted between Thailand and India for over fifty years, the trade volume between two countries has been relatively low. The average trade volume over the last five years has been US$1,400 million per year, which is only 1 per cent of Thailand's international trade volume. In the last five years Thailand has continuously had a trade deficit with India. However, during 2003–04, trade volumes increased significantly from US$1,508 in 2003 to US$2,049 million in 2004, compared with previous trade volumes which were approximately US$1,100–1,200 million. Trade expansion rates during 2003–04 were relatively high, at 27.3 per cent and 35.8 per cent respectively. While Thailand still has a trade deficit with India, the deficit value has decreased from US$231 million to US$222 million (Table 4.1).

Based on trade data in 2004, Thailand's exports to India were dominated by industrial products. Machinery and mechanical appliances, electronic machinery and equipment, plastics and articles thereof, the top-three Thailand's exports to India, were valued at US$173 million, US$135 million, and US$93 million respectively. The top-ten exports to India were all industrial products, which accounted for 75 per cent of total exports to India (Table 4.2).

On the import side, the top-ten Thai imports from India in 2004 were mostly industrial products except prepared animal fodder. Jewelry and precious metals, iron and steel and prepared animal fodder were the top three Thai imports from India. Most of the top-ten Thai imports were imported to be raw material for Thai industry, especially jewellery and precious metals which were valued at more than US$280 million. Iron and steel and prepared animal fodders were imported at levels around US$144 and 119 million respectively. The top-ten Thai imports from India accounted for 84 per cent of total Thai imports to India in 2004 (Table 4.3).

Even though both countries are not major trading partners, Thailand and India have a high potential for trade expansion. In terms of trade between Thailand and countries in South Asia, India has been the biggest import and export market for Thailand over the past five years.

Trade in services

In accordance with the General Agreement on Trade in Services (GATS), India has committed to liberalize six service sectors under the existing laws and regulations: business services, communication services, construction and related engineering services, financial services, health-related and social services, and tourism and travel-related

Table 4.1 Trade volume between Thailand and India, 2000–04

Year	*Total trade volume*			*Exports*			*Imports*			*Balance of trade (US$ millions)*
	Volume (US$ millions)	*Share*	*%*	*Volume (US$ millions)*	*Share*	*%*	*Volume (US$ millions)*	*Share*	*%*	
2000	1,122.60	0.85	–	499.7	0.72	–	622.9	1.00	–	−123.2
2001	1,154.10	0.91	2.81	483.1	0.74	−3.32	671.0	1.09	7.72	−187.9
2002	1,184.80	0.89	2.66	413.7	0.61	−14.37	771.1	1.20	14.92	−357.4
2003	1,508.50	0.97	27.32	638.6	0.80	54.36	869.9	1.16	12.81	−231.3
2004	2,049.00	1.06	35.83	913.4	0.93	43.03	1,135.60	1.20	30.54	−222.2

Note: Share = Trade between Thailand and India compared with total Thailand trade. % = Growth rate compared with previous year.
Source: Thai Customs Department.

Table 4.2 Top-ten Thailand's export products to India, 2004

	Categories	*Export volume US$ millions*	%
1	Machinery and mechanical appliances	173.24	19
2	Electronic machinery and equipment	134.92	15
3	Plastics and articles thereof	92.85	10
4	Vehicles and parts thereof	64.91	7
5	Rubber and articles thereof	62.31	7
6	Iron and Steel	46.28	5
7	Jewellery and precious metals	33.16	4
8	Man-made staple fibres	30.09	3
9	Organic chemicals	25.17	3
10	Textiles articles	24.51	3
Total		687.44	75

Note: % = Percentage of product's export volume compared with total export volume to India in 2004.
Source: Thai Customs Department.

Table 4.3 Top-ten Thailand's import products from India, 2004

Categories		*Import volume US$ millions*	%
1	Jewellery and precious metals	281.32	25
2	Iron and Steel	144.35	13
3	Prepared animal fodders	119.61	11
4	Copper and article thereof	92.26	8
5	Mineral fuels and mineral oils	90.25	8
6	Organic chemicals	75.22	7
7	Machinery and mechanical appliances	69.36	6
8	Silk	29.05	3
9	Miscellaneous chemical products	27.24	2
10	Tanning or dyeing extracts	22.91	2
Total		951.57	84

Note: % = Percentage of product's import volume compared with total import volume from India in 2004.
Source: Thai Customs Department.

services. In addition, Thailand has committed to liberalize 10 service sectors under existing laws and regulations similar to India's, including the six sectors above plus education services, environmental services, recreational cultural and sporting services, and transport services.

Both countries may in particular explore opportunities to liberalize in sectors such as tourism and travel-related services that both countries have committed to under GATS. In 2003, Indian tourists ranked 14th in the Thai tourist market, yet while more than 250,000 Indians visited Thailand, fewer than 25,000 Thais went to India. There is an opportunity for both countries to cooperate in this sector.

Investment aspect

During 1991–2002, Indian investment projects in Thailand were generally structured as joint ventures and their value was approximately US$1,000 million, the projects covering petrochemicals, medical and pharmaceutical products, textiles (rayon fibre) and steel wires and rods. Thai investments in India over the same period were of volume approximately US$800 million, and included joint venture projects in telecommunications, healthcare and tourism. As regards India's investment volume in Thailand in 2003 and 2004, a total of 5,100 million baht or about US$127 million (3519.3 million baht in 2003) from India was invested in Thailand, facilitated by the Thai Board of Investment (see Appendix 1). The majority of investment projects are small and medium, although India's investment in Thailand was ranked 10th from all countries. However, the trend of India investment in Thailand is promising and was expected to increase in 2005. The Thai Prime Minister visited India in June 2005 to persuade Indian businessmen and investors to invest in Thailand and has set up a focal point in the Board of Investment to concentrate on this matter.

Expanding economic cooperation with India

Three aspects of India make the country particularly appealing as a destination for investments and exports:

- Its **population**: Approximately 300 million people or 30 per cent of India's population are at least in the middle class or above. Indeed, India prides itself as the largest middle-class democracy in the world. This group is one of the most powerful consumer groups in the world, and anyone who can successfully cater to the Indian middle class stands to gain enormously.
- Its **worker base**: India is the high-tech hub of Asia; the country graduates more than 350,000 engineers per year. With the current

Table 4.4 Economic indicators (India and Thailand), 2003 and 2004

Economic indicators	*2003*		*2004*	
	India	*Thailand*	*India*	*Thailand*
Growth rate of GDP (%)	7.3	6.7	7.4	7.2
Growth rate of per capita GDP (%)	5.5	5.8	5.7	6.4
Inflation rate (whole price index)	5.3	1.8	5	2.4
Fiscal balance	−11	0.6	−10	−0.1
Merchandise export growth (% per year)	15.1	18.6	16.1	14
Merchandise import growth (% per year)	19.7	17.1	18.7	17.8
Current account balance/GDP	0.7	5.6	0.3	3.9
External debt/GDP	18	15	16	13.5
Foreign direct investment (US$ million)	3,585	954	NA	NA

Source: *Asian Development Outlook* (2004).

low labour costs, and the high percentage of English speakers, India is a prime destination for investments in high-tech industries and service outsourcing.

- Its **economy**: India's economic growth rate is approximately 7 per cent, which in Asia is second only to China. This high growth rate, if maintained consistently, will propel India into the forefront of global economic powers within a short time. However, in terms of fiscal balance, India's deficit is 10 per cent of GDP, and this deficit is a critical factor which could affect the stability of India's economy in the long run. To maintain the high growth rate, the government will have to promote steady investment and trade expansion, and reign-in unnecessary spending, keeping inflation in check.

Economic overview

Economic indicators for India and Thailand in 2003 and 2004 are shown in Table 4.4.

Thailand's trade and investment policies and opportunities

Thailand is committed to liberalizing trade and encouraging economic growth. Thailand is well-regarded for having a tolerant society that is friendly to foreigners and foreign businesses. Thailand is ranked

20th for ease of doing business in the World Bank's evaluation for doing business worldwide in 2006. Thailand provides basic investment privileges and both tax and non-tax incentives.

Thailand targets a number of potential high-growth and new-growth sectors: agro-industry; food and rubber products; fashion; jewellery; garments; leather; automotive; electronics and ICT; alternative energy; and high-value added services.

Thailand is therefore strategically placed as a gateway to India from Southeast Asia and the rest of the Pacific Rim for the following reasons:

Thailand as a transportation link between India and East Asia

Ground transportation: India is right on the border of ASEAN. India's neighbouring countries in the north-east are Myanmar and China, while the southern peninsula extends into the Indian Ocean. The Thailand–Myanmar–India link route will serve as the cargo transportation road between India and ASEAN countries, and Thailand will be a significant trade strategic connector between India and ASEAN countries. The project has been clearly mapped out in the ASEAN–India Partnership for Peace, Progress and Shared Prosperity plan, through which Thailand will benefit and become a Thai–China–India trade centre.

Overseas transportation: Ranong port was opened in 2003, and is Thailand's Andaman coastal strategic port supporting South Asia and European countries' trade growth. Currently, the one-way trip for freight from Bangkok to South Asia via Malaysia and Singapore takes 25 days, which can be shortened to only 4–7 days via Ranong port, representing an enormous saving on freight costs. It is expected that the Thai government will announce the upgrade of Ranong port to an international system port in 2006.

Furthermore, Ranong port is Thailand's transportation connector from abroad and can link to other areas such as Chiang Saen port in the north by road the southern and central part of China by boat or to Indochina countries.

Air transportation: Thailand has signed air contracts with India for various routes to accommodate commercial flights with India. According to India's Look East policy, Thailand will be a gateway that connects India with East Asian countries. Thai Airways offers routes to Calcutta, Delhi, Mumbai, Chennai and Bangalore, and, furthermore,

Thailand opened its new Suvarnabhumi international airport in 2006 which provides opportunities to expand routes to India and other countries.

Thailand is an easy country to do business in

Starting a business involves a great deal of paperwork, and much bureaucratic red tape. Afterwards, business owners have to comply with various regulations and rules set out by local authorities. Thus, the same business may have different levels of cost in different countries.

The World Bank has evaluated 155 countries on the ease of doing business, using criteria such as ease in enforcing a contract, ease in hiring and firing workers, and so on, as a baseline for comparison. Thailand was ranked in the top-20 for 2006, with only three Asian countries ranked higher: Singapore (2nd), Hong Kong (7th), and Japan (10th).

Thailand's government has for decades realized the importance of foreign investment as an engine for economic growth, and has relentlessly promoted Thailand as an investment destination. Investment promotions are given to foreign firms wishing to establish production centres in Thailand, and the legal code has been overhauled to be more in line with international standards.

The general cost of doing business in Thailand is also very low compared to other countries in the region, and the government has always been keen to promote new investments in Thailand (see Appendix 2). As such, Thailand has become the choice for regional headquarters for many international firms.

Thailand has a liberal investment regime

It is very easy to set up a manufacturing base in Thailand. The country does not have foreign equity limits in the manufacturing sector, and there are no export on local-content requirements.

The Board of Investment also grants generous tax breaks for qualified applicants, who wish to set up a manufacturing base for exports. The tax incentives include a corporate income-tax holiday for up to eight years, and import-duty exemptions for raw materials and machinery. This liberal investment structure has resulted in many international companies relocating their manufacturing bases to Thailand.

Thailand is located in a strategic gateway and has negotiated many FTAs

Geographically, Thailand has the virtue of being near to almost every country in Asia. Flights from Europe stopover at Bangkok airport before flying on to Australia and New Zealand, and many businessmen from East Asia stop in Thailand before continuing their journey onto South Asia and the Middle East. Thailand is strategically situated in Asia, and can be a gateway to the rest of Asia.

Moreover, Thailand has or is in the process of negotiating various FTA agreements with other Asian countries, and once most of these agreements are in place Thailand will have one of the lowest taxes in the region and can truly become a trading hub for Asia.

As for India, currently Thailand is a party to three frameworks to liberalize trading with India. These three frameworks are:

1 **The Framework Agreement for Establishing a Free Trade Area between Thailand and India**. This Agreement was signed by Ministers of Commerce from both countries on 9 October 2003, and is considered a crucial step in trade enhancement between Thailand and India.

  According to the framework agreement, initially Thailand and India agreed to eliminate tariffs on 82 items of fast-track products for the three years from 1 September 2004 to 1 September 2006. The 82 items are listed in Appendix 3.

  Following the implementation of 82 EHS products since September 2004, the trade in those products expanded by 93.7 per cent. Exports increased by 135 per cent and imports by approximately 13 per cent. Thailand now has a trade surplus with India.

Table 4.5 Tariff reduction and elimination for products covered under the Early Harvest Scheme (EHS)

Period	*Tariff reduction on applied MFN tariff rates as of 1 January 2004*
1 September 2004–31 August 2005	50%
1 September 2005–31 August 2006	75%
1 September 2006	100%

The top export EHS products from Thailand to India are polycarbonates, televisions, cathode-ray tubes and air conditioners, which grew by 666 per cent, 133.4 per cent, 397.6 per cent, and 150 per cent, respectively.

On the import side, the top import EHS products from India are gearboxes, aluminum (not alloyed), and jewellery and parts. The growth rates of these products were 1,734.7 per cent, 136.1 per cent and 205.7 per cent respectively over the period.

The remaining products of more than 5,000 items will be further discussed and negotiated. Negotiation about trade in services and investment started in January 2004.

Economic cooperation is to be enhanced in various ways as follows: through trade facilitation; promotion of trade and investment; and cooperation in agriculture, fisheries and aquaculture; in information and communications technology; space technology; biotechnology; finance and banking; tourism; infrastructure development; health care; construction; education; and government procurement.

Currently, the 82 items under the Early Harvest Scheme create mutual benefits of trade expansion for both Thailand and India. The value of the 82 EHS items trade in the 11 months September 2004–July 2005 increased by approximately US$283 million and about 64 per cent on the previous year (September 2003–July 2004).

The Thai–India FTA negotiation is continuously being discussed on important issues such as tariff modality, sensitive list and rules of origin.

Table 4.6 Trade in 82 EHS products Jan–Oct 2005

	2004 (Jan–Oct) before EHS	*2005 (Jan–Oct)*	*% increase 2005/2004*
Total trade (US$ million)	175.9	340.7	+93.7%
Export (US$ million)	116.3	273.5	+135.2%
Import (US$ million)	59.6	67.2	+12.7%
Balance of trade (US$ million)	56.7	206.3	+263.9%

2 **The Framework Agreement on Comprehensive Economic Cooperation between ASEAN and India.** ASEAN countries and India leaders signed a framework agreement for economic cooperation on 8 October 2003 at Bali Indonesia. The key elements cover trade in goods, services and investment as well as other areas of economic cooperation. The main topics include three groups of trade tariffs reduction and elimination:

(a) Fast-track products (Early Harvest Programme (EHP). There are 105 items; the programme started on 1 November 2004 and tariffs were to be reduced to 0% by 31 October 2007 (ASEAN and India later agreed not to pursue the EHP).
(b) Normal track products. Tariffs were to be reduced or eliminated over a period from: 1 Jan. 2006 to 31 Dec. 2011 for ASEAN-6 and India; from 1 Jan. 2006 to 31 Dec. 2016 for the Philippines and India; from 1 Jan. 2006 to 31 Dec. 2011 for India; and from 1 Jan. 2006 to 31 Dec. 2016 for CLMV.
(c) Sensitive track products. Tariffs are to be reduced/eliminated within timeframes to be mutually agreed between the parties.

Trade in services and investment was to be negotiated in 2005 and concluded within 2007.

Economic cooperation will be enhanced in various ways as follows: trade facilitation, promotion of trade and investment, cooperation in agriculture, services, energy, science and technology, transportation and basic infrastructure.

Currently, FTAs on trade in goods are still under negotiation on modality of tariff reduction/elimination, products in the sensitive list and the Rules of Origin (ROO). Framework Agreement may need to be amended due to the ROO negotiations as follows:

- ASEAN and India agreed not to pursue EHP from December 2005.
- Negotiations on trade in goods were extended from 30 June 2005 to 30 June 2006.
- Starting date of tariff reduction was extended from 1 January 2006 to 1 January 2007.
- Base rate of tariff reduction was changed from 'MFN Applied Rate as of 1 July 2004' to '1 July 2005'.

- Dispute Settlement Mechanism (DSM) was due to be set up by 30 September 2006.

3 **The Framework Agreement on the BIMSTEC Free Trade Area.** This agreement for establishing a free trade area of BIMSTEC was signed by ministers of commerce from all member countries except Bangladesh on 8 February 2004 in Phuket, Thailand. Later on, Bangladesh also signed the agreement as a founding member.

According to the free trade area agreement of BIMSTEC, the tariff reduction product list is divided into two tracks, a fast track and a normal track, and Table 4.7 shows the tariff reduction timeframes for these.

Negative listed products will be negotiated on the ceiling of the product, and negotiations on trade in services and investment was scheduled to be concluded by 2007. Economic cooperation is to be enhanced in various ways as follows: cooperation in the already identified sectors of technology, transportation and communication, energy, tourism, fisheries, customs cooperation, trade finance, e-commerce, business visas and travel facilitation.

Up to December 2005 a total of nine BIMSTEC meetings had been convened, the last on 7–13 November 2005 in India. Tariff modalities were concluded but the fast-track and normal-track lists, and a negative list and rules of origin are still being negotiated.

Table 4.7 Fast track and normal track tariff reduction timeframes

Countries	*For developing countries*	*For least developed countries (LDCs)*
India, Sri Lanka and Thailand		
Fast track	1 July 2006–30 June 2009	1 July 2006–30 June 2007
Normal track	1 July 2007–30 June 2012	1 July 2007–30 June 2010
Bhutan, Myanmar, Bangladesh and Nepal		
Fast track	1 July 2006–30 June 2011	1 July 2006–30 June 2009
Normal track	1 July 2007–30 June 2017	1 July 2007–30 June 2015

Implications for the Asian community

India's rise to the status of an economic powerhouse is inevitable in the long run. The country has a huge middle class who are relatively sophisticated; its highly trained and English-speaking population has secured the migration of many high-paying service jobs into the country; the government is democratic and relatively stable; and the economy has grown at a healthy pace in recent years. The Indian market is a well of huge untapped potential.

As such, Asian countries view India with ambiguity. On the one hand, India competes with others as a destination for foreign direct investment. One can easily observe this phenomenon in the birth of the new high-tech cities of India, which is tapping into the market for highly trained technicians and engineers who are inexpensive to hire and are of high quality. Many corporations are relocating their back-office service centres to India, which also has the side-effect of creating tensions between India and major powers such as the United States. In a sense this is a zero-sum game, in which capital is allocated to countries which can best utilize the capital. In this respect, India has become very efficient and so can capture a large share of capital movements, perhaps even at the expense of its neighbours.

On the other hand, India represents a huge opportunity as a potential market for consumption. Already, India has a large pool of aspiring sophisticated middle-class citizens, well-versed in the jargon of the latest fashions and global consumer culture and entertainment. And as the economy of India grows and vast numbers of the population are lifted out of poverty, more people will reach the middle class. There is a huge market in the making to satisfy current consumers and new consumers who are not yet on the radar screen today.

Since the rise of India is inevitable, India's Asian neighbours must position themselves to benefit from having India as a partner. As we have already seen, Asian countries are negotiating new trade agreements with India and encouraging more cultural and economic exchanges. Asian countries will definitely compete with India for new investment dollars, but at the same time they will also reap benefits from accessing the vast untapped market. India may become a rising tide that lifts all boats.

Prospects and challenges

At present, although both countries are not major trade partners, the establishment of a free trade area has fostered trade flow. As result of the open market in early harvest products, the total trade volume between the two countries was about US$2,303 million in the first nine months of 2005, an increase of 32.5 per cent over the first nine months of 2004 and reached nearly US$2,500 million at the end of year 2005. The trade volume between Thailand and India is expected to double by 2009.

By 2010 Thailand will have realized benefits from tariff concessions in ASEAN and FTAs between Thailand and India. These benefits will attract FDI to enhance market access in Asia and Thailand's FTA partners. In FTAs between Thailand and India, both sides will have mutual benefits in various industries such as jewellery, automotive products and electronics. Partnership is significant in terms of investment enhancement, especially for small and medium-sized industries.

Moreover, the Thailand and India Free Trade Area, the ASEAN–India Free Trade Area and the BIMSTEC Free Trade Area are under negotiations. However Thailand and India still have some difficulties which both sides need to address. The rules of origin, the concept of reciprocity, and the number of products in the sensitive list are the most critical issues that both sides need to clarify in order to clearly understand each other's attitudes and positions.

Due to the current high tariff rates, the loss of tariff revenue from the FTA agreements will need to be considered. India has a large number of poor people that need to be taken care of and any loss of government revenue could mean catastrophic cuts in basic services to the poor. Therefore, there are some restrictions in the opening of its market and time is needed to adjust. Both sides need to be flexible with each other and understand their limitations in order to overcome the critical issues.

In addition, cooperation between Thailand and India in other aspects must be promoted simultaneously. According to the Global Competitiveness Index, the World Economic Forum ranked India at 50th position in terms of country competitiveness in 2005. India had moved up five places from the previous year due to technology development, while Thailand dropped two places from 34th to 36th. Investment-enhancement in terms of partnership systems is significant, especially for small and medium-sized industries. Both countries have a high potential from private joint ventures between the two countries or to act as each other's supply chain. India's strong points are in information technology and healthcare, and knowledge exchange will mutually benefit both countries. Nevertheless, social and cultural cooperation cannot be neglected, and social and cultural understanding will strengthen trade and economic relations.

Lastly, the most challenging aspect of any free trade framework is the question of distribution. Amartya Sen, the eminent Indian economist, cautions that the benefits of free trade can only make sense if the gains of free trade are distributed equitably and not accrued disproportionately to one group of people. If everyone is entitled to benefit equally from free trade, then no one must be less equal than others.

Conclusion

To use a common expression, we believe that India is now, more than anytime in modern history, poised to take its rightful place in the global trade arena, and the effect on Asia and the world will be immense once the Indian market fully opens up. The free trade frameworks with ASEAN and Thailand are the first steps among many other steps towards a more global integration. Thailand stands to benefit from the free trade framework, and we believe that with our proximity to India, and the long history of cultural exchanges, Thailand can also serve as one of the gateways to India.

Appendix 1: foreign investment in Thailand, 2002–04

Table 4.8 Foreign investment in Thailand from major countries (=10%; baht millions)

Country	*Net applications*						*Applications approved*					
	2002		*2003*		*2004*		*2002*		*2003*		*2004*	
	No.	*Total Invest.*	*No.*	*Total Invest.*	*No.*	*Total Invest.*	*No.*	*Total Invest.*	*No.*	*Total Invest.*	*No.*	*Total Invest.*
Total Investment	844	264,746	1,029	319,036	1,168	636,095	721	162,532	841	285,582	1,227	600,729
Total Foreign Investment	560	178,620	668	248,692	749	307,008	483	99,617	563	212,689	784	317,291
100% Foreign Investment	292	102,795	305	106,183	394	109,627	273	53,434	305	104,487	377	127,942
Asia												
Japan	251	71,881	316	106,374	340	101,856	215	38,398	260	97,597	350	125,932
Asian NIEs												
• Taiwan	55	41,472	67	7,931	61	9,305	41	2,706	57	13,553	53	10,607
• Hong Kong	13	11,515	16	12,439	18	2,590	5	1,585	14	3,591	23	14,317
• Korea	37	2,956	48	6,539	29	2,922	33	3,213	40	3,506	42	6,631
• Singapore	40	3,964	62	14,581	81	22,298	40	13,103	36	6,730	74	18,239
PRC	12	2,081	16	2,333	30	3,483	7	379	11	1,465	20	4,433
Malaysia	30	2,343	33	5,813	48	13,235	23	1,676	30	4,374	39	11,937
Indonesia	2	140	2	241	4	1,043	2	139	2	534	5	1,253
Philippines	2	154	3	525	3	703	1	30	3	645	2	26
India	7	145	13	3,445	20	2,096	5	92	11	3,519	19	1,615

(Continued)

Table 4.8 (Continued)

Country	*Net applications*						*Applications approved*					
	2002		*2003*		*2004*		*2002*		*2003*		*2004*	
	No.	*Total nvest.*	*No.*	*Total Invest.*	*No.*	*Total Invest.*	*No.*	*Total Invest.*	*No.*	*Total Invest.*	*No.*	*Total Invest.*
North America												
USA	35	8,440	43	47,446	39	35,223	37	11,113	40	24,574	37	30,397
Canada	4	297	4	221	4	581	2	93	2	236	5	147
Australia												
Australia	3	430	15	6,284	14	552	11	726	9	4,988	14	1,670
European Union	66	13,304	74	36,431	94	32,066	65	16,259	62	24,913	75	30,430
All Europe	78	16,770	77	39,738	104	37,601	78	20,437	70	28,311	81	32,980
• UK	21	9,946	19	20,308	23	2,019	15	11,237	14	30,513	17	2,491
• Germany	14	801	17	814	21	5,044	19	2,140	12	413	15	913
• Switzerland	12	2,966	3	705	8	5,159	12d	3,727	7	898	7	2,841
• France	10	716	10	764	12	949	9	543	13	1,321	11	784
• Belgium	2	94	8	3,767	8	5,108	3	73	5	454	7	8,278
• Italy	3	460	2	125	4	571	2	633	3	98	3	424
• Netherlands	10	950	9	9,624	15	10,850	10	858	3	819	14	16,100

Total Investment	796	221,682	717	228,730	1,053	371,298	626	203,720	251	74,582	279	83,036
Total Foreign Investment	541	166,684	484	168,943	654	254,626	413	146,920	154	50,778	178	49,786
100% Foreign Investment	263	61,507	231	68,693	324	103,144	204	87,417	60	9,933	78	13,830
Asia												
Japan	246	66,154	236	80,099	334	105,021	180	54,786	54	31,774	74	22,144
Asian NIEs												
• Taiwan	40	3,010	43	12,803	53	9,369	54	9,514	16	9,634	16	2,659
• Hong Kong	10	1,834	10	2,401	25	6,821	19	4,236	8	574	3	975
• Korea	30	2,990	36	1,752	46	7,415	11	1,466	4	219	2	100
• Singapore	42	13,041	41	9,276	60	20,200	44	11,276	12	3,934	16	1,794
PRC	7	4,504	5	467	11	2,373	1	55	1	5	3	1,212
Malaysia	26	26,935	25	4,041	27	7,251	19	2,187	10	3,292	8	1,219
Indonesia	2	139	–	–	2	251	3	94	1	190	0	0
Philippines	2	65	–	–	4	647	–	–	–	–	0	0
India	7	1,378	10	1,617	7	367	3	141	–	–	2	273

(Continued)

Table 4.8 (Continued)

Country	*Promotion certificates issued*						*Start-ups*					
	2002		*2003*		*2004*		*2002*		*2003*		*2004*	
	No.	*Total Invest.*	*No.*	*Total Invest.*	*No.*	*Total Invest.*	*No.*	*Total Invest.*	*No.*	*Total Invest.*	*No.*	*Total Invest.*
North America												
USA	37	11,061	33	24,136	31	29,803	33	26,977	9	2,389	8	1,964
Canada	4	134	3	551	4	253	4	31	2	8	1	4
Australia												
Australia	13	1,192	7	784	13	5,091	6	1,263	3	108	2	319
European Union	57	14,926	55	15,378	60	43,367	58	43,317	34	10,337	41	8,894
All Europe	72	21,166	62	16,016	65	46,815	60	45,007	37	11,207	45	9,340
• UK	18	10,822	13	4,956	13	18,859	13	1,450	7	628	9	1,207
• Germany	13	1,406	12	5,743	8	887	8	1,301	9	329	12	731
• Switzerland	14	5,862	7	638	5	1,165	7	1,190	3	870	5	600
• France	9	446	8	424	11	791	9	350	3	7,834	8	4,932
• Belgium	1	4	4	368	5	4,110	5	716	1	39	3	168
• Italy	1	100	2	477	2	343	1	112	3	194	2	573
• Netherlands	9	1,434	6	2,030	11	15,583	11	38,023	7	1,234	6	1,203

Appendix 2: doing business in Thailand

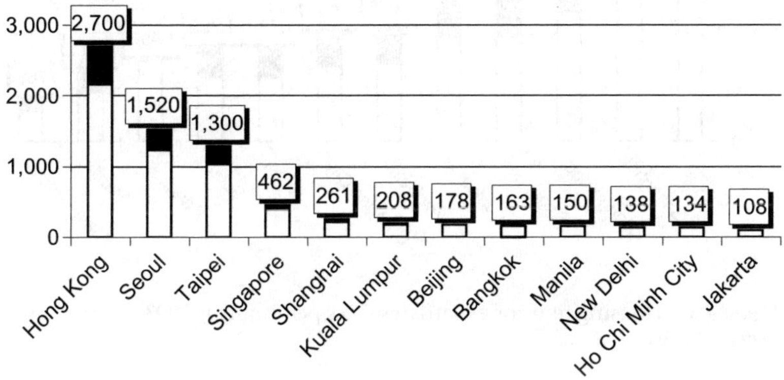

Figure 4.1 Monthly wages of industry workers (US$), 2003
Source: JETRO.

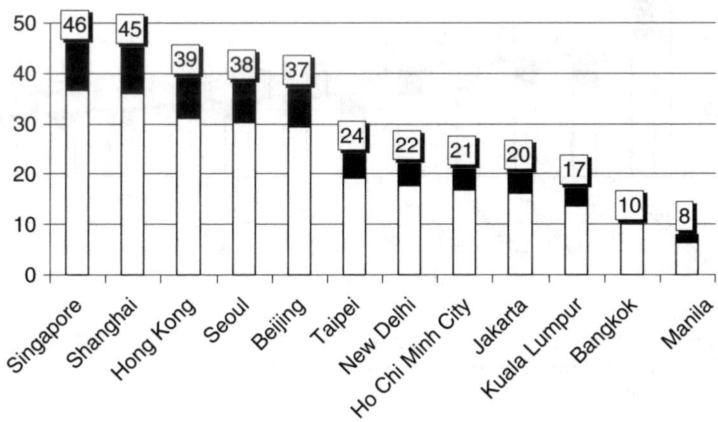

Figure 4.2 Office rent monthly per square metre (US$), 2003
Source: JETRO.

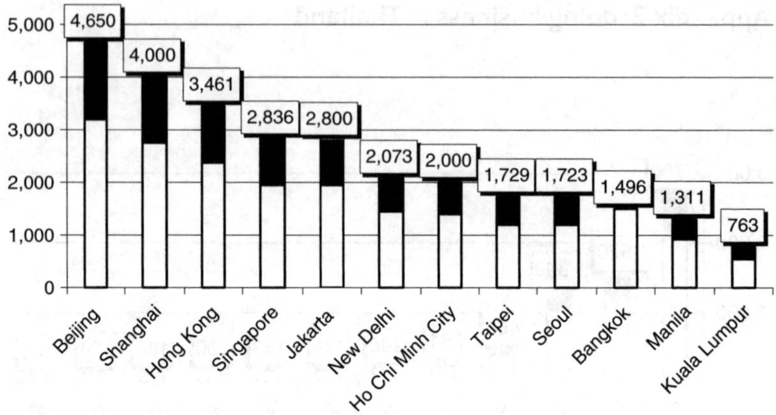

Figure 4.3 Housing rent for expatriates (US$ per month), 2003
Source: JETRO.

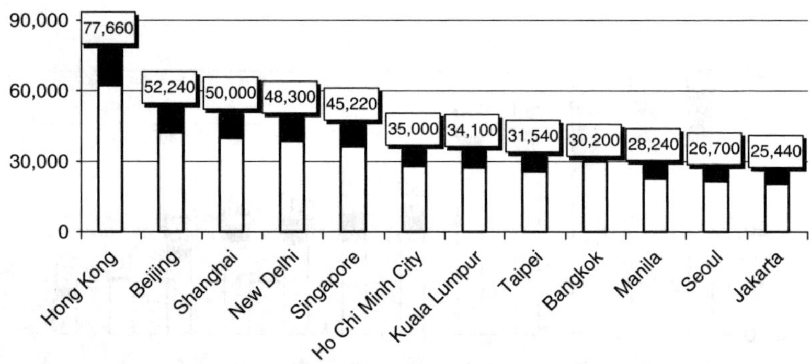

Figure 4.4 Electricity rate for business use (US$) per month, 2003 (at contracted power: 2,000 kW, amount of use: 500,000 kWh)
Source: JETRO.

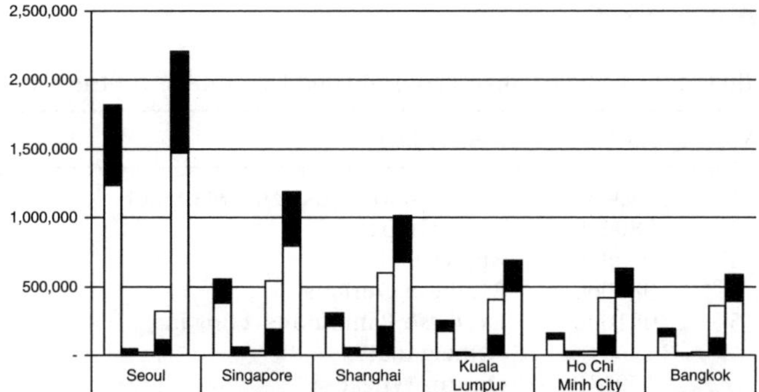

	Seoul	Singapore	Shanghai	Kuala Lumpur	Ho Chi Minh City	Bangkok
100 workers on payroll	1,824,000	554,400	313,200	249,600	160,800	105,600
Office 100 square meters	45,600	55,200	54,000	20,400	25,200	12,000
House rent for one expatriate	20,676	34,032	48,000	9,156	24,000	17,952
Average electricity usage	320,400	542,640	600,000	409,200	420,000	362,400
Total	2,210,676	1,186,272	1,015,200	688,356	630,000	587,952

Figure 4.5 Calculation example of selected annual cost (US$), 2003.
Source: JETRO.

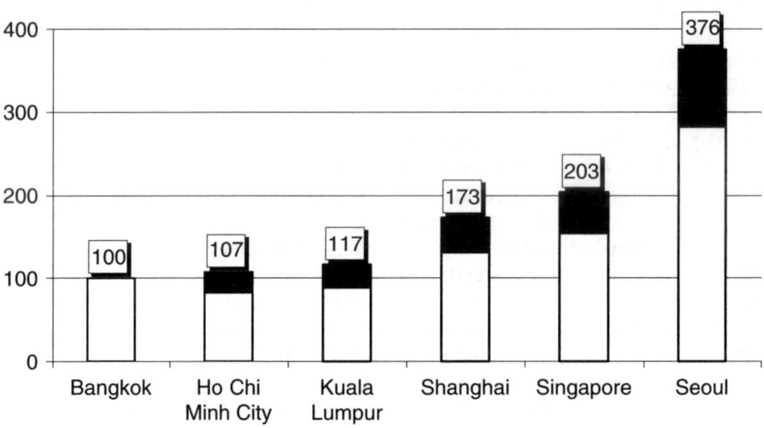

Figure 4.6 Cost structure index, 2003 (Bangkok = 100)
Source: JETRO.

Appendix 3

Table 4.9 India–Thailand consolidated list of items for the EHS

No.	*HS.*	*Descriptions*
1	080450	Ex. Fresh Mangosteens, Mangoes
2	080610	Fresh Grapes
3	080810	Apples
4	081060	Ex. Fresh Durians
5	081090	Ex. Fresh Rambutans, Longans, Pomegranates
6	100110	Durum Wheat
7	100190	Other Wheat And Meslin
8	160411	Salmon, Whole or in Pices but not Minced, Prepared or Preserved
9	160413	Sardines, Sardenella and Brisling or Sprats, Whole or in Pieces but not Minced, Prepared or Preserved
10	160415	Mackeral Whole or in Pieces but not Minced, Prepared or Preserved
11	160510	Crab Prepared or Preserved
12	250100	Salt (Incl Table Salt & Denatrd Salt) & Pure Sodium Chloride W/N AQS Soln Sea WTR
13	261000	Chromium Ores & Concentrates
14	281119	Other Inorganic Acids
15	281820	Other Aluminium Oxide
16	281830	Aluminium Hydroxide
17	291739	Other Aromatic Polycarboxylic Acids their Anhydrides Halides Peroxides Peroxyacids & their Derivatives
18	390690	Other Acrylic Polymers in Primary Forms.
19	390710	Polyacetals in Primary Forms.
20	390730	Epoxide Resins in Primary Forms.
21	390740	Polycarbonates in Primary Forms.
22	390799	Saturated Polyallyl Esters and Other Saturated Pol
23	390810	Polyamide-6,-11,-12,-6,6,-6,9,-6,10 OR -6,12,IN Primary Forms
24	390890	Other Polyamides in Primary Forms.
25	390950	Polyurethanes in Primary Forms.
26	391990	Other Self-Adhesive Plates, Sheets, Film, Foil, Tape, Strip and other Flat Shapes of Plastics
27	441219	Other Plywood Comsstng only Sheets of Wood of Thickness of each Sheet NT Excd 6 mm

(Continued)

Table 4.9 (Continued)

No.	*HS.*	*Descriptions*
28	710310	Precious Stones (other than Diamonds) and Semi-Precious Stones, Unworked or Simply Sawn or Roughly Shaped
29	710490	Other Synthetic or Reconstructed Precious or Semi-Precious Stones
30	710510	Dust and Powder of Diamonds
31	711319	Articles of Jewellery and Parts thereof, of other Precious Metal, whether or not Plated or Clad with Precious Metal
32	720150	Alloy Pig Iron: Spiegeleisen
33	720711	Products Containing by Weight < 0.25% Carbon, of Rectangular (Incl Sqr) Crs-Sctn; Wdth < Twice the Thickness
34	720719	Other Products Containing by Weight < 0.25% of Carbon
35	722619	Flt-Rold Products of Silicon Electrical Steel other than Grain-Oriented
36	722990	Other Wire
37	730792	Threaded Elbows, Bends and Sleeves of Iron or Steel
38	732020	Helical Springs, of Iron or Steel
39	732690	Other Articles of Iron or Steel Wire, not Forged
40	760110	Aluminum, not Alloyed
41	760120	Aluminum Alloys
42	840490	Parts of the Items of 840410 & 840420
43	840991	Parts Suitable for Use Solely or Principally with Spark-Ignition Internal Combustion Piston Engines
44	841360	Other Rotary Positive Displacement Pumps
45	841381	Other Pumps
46	841451	Table, Floor, Wall, Window, Ceiling/Roof Fans, with Self-Contained Electric Motor of Output < =125W
47	841459	Other Fans
48	841490	Parts of Air/Vaccum Pumps, Compressors & Fans
49	841510	Window/Wall Types Self-Contained Air Conditioning Machines
50	841821	Compression-Type Refrigerators, Household
51	841990	Parts of Machinery, Plant/Laboratory Equipment etc of the Items of Hdg 8419
52	842199	Other Parts of Filtering/Purifying Machinery
53	842390	Weighing Machine Weights & Parts of the Machinery

(Continued)

Table 4.9 (Continued)

No.	*HS.*	*Descriptions*
54	842549	Jacks, Hoists, of a Kind used for Raising Vehicles
55	843221	Disc Harrows
56	843780	Other Machinery for Clng, Srtng/Gradng Seeds
57	844820	Parts & Accessors of Machines of Hdg. No.8444/Of their Auxlry Machinery
58	844833	Spindles, Spindle Flyers,Spinning Rings and Ring Travellers
59	847141	Other Digital Automatic Data Processing Machns Comprisng in Samehousing a Centralprocessing Unit & Input & Output Unit, Wh/Not Combined
60	847190	Other
61	847290	Other Office Machines
62	847751	Machinery for Moulding/Retreadng Pneumatic Types or for Moulding/Otherwise Forming Inner Tubes
63	847989	Other Mchn &Mchncl Applncs of Hdg 8479
64	847990	Parts of Machines of Hdg 8479
65	848079	Other Moulds for Rubber/Plastics
66	848180	Other Appliances for Pipes, Boiler Shells, Tanks, Vats or the Like
67	848210	Ball Bearings
68	848350	Flywheels and Pulleys, including Pulley Blocks
69	850431	Other Transformers having a Power Handling Capacity not Excdng 1 Kva
70	851220	Other Lighting or Visual Signalling Equipment
71	851711	Line Telephone Set with Cordless Hand Sets.
72	851790	Parts of Telephonic/Telegraphic Apparatus
73	852390	Other Prepared Unrecorded Media
74	852812	Receptn Aparts for TV etc Colour
75	852910	Aerials & Aerials Reflectors of all Kinds Parts Suitable for use therewith
76	853400	Printed Circuits
77	854011	Cathode-Ray TV Picture Tubes, Including Video Monitor-Cathode-Ray Tubes-Colour
78	870840	Gear Boxes
79	903289	Other Atmtc Rgltng/Cntrlng Instruments&Apparatus
80	903290	Parts and Accessories of Instruments of 9032
81	910211	Wrist-Watches, Electrily Operated,W/N Incrprtng Stop-Watch Fclty with Mchncl Display only
82	940190	Parts of Seats, whether or not Convertible into Beds

References

Asia Least-Cost Greenhouse Gas Abatement Strategy: India, ADB, United Nations Development Programme, October 1998.
An Analysis of the Impacts of Establishment of the Thailand–India Free Trade Area, Ministry of Commerce, Chulalongkorn, August 2003.
Asian Development Outlook, 2004.
Thailand Economic Monitors, World Bank Thailand Office, November 2004.
International Financial Statistics, International Monetary Fund, May 2005.
India Today, 16 August 2004.

Agreements

Framework Agreement for Establishing a Free Trade Area between Thailand and India.
Framework Agreement on Comprehensive Economic Cooperation between The Association of South East Asian Nations and the Republic of India.
Framework Agreement on the BIMSTEC Free Trade Area.

Internet sites

http://www.mfa.go.th
http://www.moc.go.th
http://www.aseansec.org
http://www.customs.go.th
http://www.ficci.com
http://www.commerce.nic.in
http://www.boi.go.th
http://www.mot.go.th
http://www.nesdb.go.th
http://www.weforum.org

5
The Position of India in the Asian Economy: Progress of Economic Integration and Poverty Alleviation

Shuji Uchikawa

Introduction

In 1991, India faced a balance of payments crisis. The Gulf War had led to a sharp increase in world oil prices, and import bills rapidly rose while trade deficits widened. Foreign currency assets had declined to Rs24 billion at the end of June 1991, barely enough to finance two weeks of imports. The government not only took recourse to the IMF by drawing twice, but also changed import substitution oriented policies, which had been maintained since independence. The change of policies is seen as economic reform.

Economic reforms have had various impacts on the national economy, and the purpose of this chapter is to examine the impact of globalization on the Indian economy. Economic reforms have proved a turning point in India gradually adjusting to globalization. Many regulations on investment have been withdrawn, and the role of the private sector has become more important. Inflow of foreign direct investment has increased, and IT industry has taken advantage of globalization and has grown due to a rapid increase of service exports. The development of the IT industry has contributed to an improvement of India's balance of payments. It has promoted not only service exports but also private remittances from developed countries. India is enjoying the benefits of globalization. The present focus is not whether globalization is good or bad, but how to adjust to globalization, minimizing the reverse affects of globalization.

Although stable economic growth has been maintained, the problem of poverty has not been solved. Poverty alleviation after economic reforms is a focus. The trickle-down effects of economic growth have been pointed out by Fujita (2002). The poverty ratio has dropped from 54.9 per cent in 1973 to 26.1 per cent in 1999, but the population below the poverty line remained above 250 million even in 1999. As poverty is still a big issue in India, the Government of India must maintain its stance to protect small farmers. The government imposes a high customs tariff on palm oil from Malaysia and Indonesia, in order to protect small cultivators of oil seeds in unirrigated areas. The economic integration of India's economy with ASEAN depends on the progress of poverty alleviation.

Economic reforms and the rise of the service sector

The Indian National Congress took the reins of government after its victory in the national elections of 1991. Since then the government has changed economic policies which had been based on an import substitution strategy, and there have been six main points of reforms.

First, exchange rates have shifted to a floating system. The rupee was devalued in 1991, and in 1992 a dual exchange rate regime which consisted of official and market exchange rates was introduced under a Liberalized Exchange Rate Management System. Moreover, the exchange rate was unified and exchange restrictions on imports were removed through the abolition of foreign exchange budgeting in 1993. In August 1994, the final step towards current account convertibility was taken by acceptance of the obligations under Article VIII of the IMF, under which India was committed to forsake the use of exchange restrictions on current international transactions as an instrument in managing its balance of payments. The changes of exchange rate policies caused the exchange rate of the rupee to depreciate against the US dollar from Rs 24.5 per US dollar in 1991 to Rs 47.7 in 2001.

Second, the industrial licensing regulation which had regulated investment to the manufacturing sector has been swept away since 1991. Industrial licensing was required from the central government to establish new industrial undertakings and to manufacture new items. It was abolished for all industries except 18 specified industries, and in 2005 only five industries were under compulsory licensing mainly on account of environmental, safety and strategic considerations. Those industries are distribution and brewing of alcoholic drinks, cigars and tobacco; electronic, aerospace and defence equipment; industrial explosives; hazardous chemicals; and drugs and pharmaceuticals.

Third, the private sector has been allowed to enter into the sector reserved for public-sector undertakings. In many industries, particularly heavy industries, public-sector undertakings had dominated. The statement of industrial policy limited industries to be reserved for the public sector to eight industries, and by 2005 only three industries – atomic energy, substances related to atomic energy, and railway transport – were reserved.

Fourth, financial sector reforms, including banking sector and capital market reforms started. The profitability of public-sector banks had deteriorated under the control of interest rates, priority-sector lending[1] and regulations of new entry before 1992, and non-performing assets became serious issues. As interest rates were controlled by the central bank, bank rate operations had not been effective; financial policies had depended on the operation of a statutory liquidity ratio (SLR) and cash reserve ratio (CRR). Bank funds were obliged to invest in government approved securities up to the level of the SLR, which had been kept at high rates to finance budgetary deficits. After 1992, regulation on interest rates has been liberalized gradually and SLR and CRR have been reduced, and the entry of private and foreign banks was permitted. In 1992 the Securities and Exchange Board of India (SEBI) Act replaced the Capital Issues Act of the late 1940s. Prior to 1992, the government very closely regulated the primary market in almost every aspect. Now companies were free to approach the capital market after they got clearance from SEBI. The total amount of new capital issues by non-government public limited companies including preference shares and debentures at 1981–82 prices jumped from Rs29,270 million in 1991–92 to Rs98,750 million in 1994–95.

Fifth, import quantity restrictions were phased out and import duty rates were reduced after India ratified the WTO in 1994. The peak rate of customs tariffs for non-agricultural products was reduced from 110 per cent in 1992–93 to 15 per cent in 2005–06.

Sixth, the policy towards foreign direct investment (FDI) was liberalized in 1991 to permit automatic approval for FDI up to 51 per cent equity in the priority industries. This was the turning point for foreign direct investment policies because the government now allowed foreign companies to control home fims.

The economic reforms induced an investment boom in the manufacturing sector in the mid-1990s (Figure 5.1). Abolition of industrial licensing encouraged investment in consumer durable goods to meet the pent-up demand under import-substitution policies before the economic reforms (Chandrasekar, 1996). The boom spread over not only consumer durable goods industries but also consumer non-durable goods, intermediate goods and capital goods industries in the manufacturing sector. As a result, the organized manufacturing sector (employing 10 or more workers and using power, and employing 20 or more workers without using power), increased rapidly after 1995. As investment increased, production also increased. The manufacturing sector maintained growth rates at about 10 per cent in the mid-1990s, but the investment boom had little impact on agriculture and electricity, gas and water supply. The impact was also limited in the transport, storage and communication, and financial, insurance and business service sectors.

Although the investment boom for the manufacturing sector was over by the end of the 1990s, investment in the service sector has increased since the end of the 1990s, with investment in community, social and personal services increasing steadily from 1991. The level of investment at 1993–94 prices increased by a factor of 2.5 between 1991–92 and 2003–04. As a result, total gross fixed capital formation

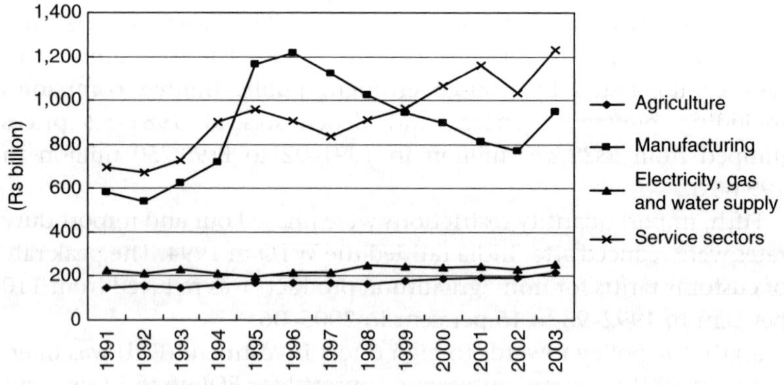

Figure 5.1 Gross fixed capital formation at 1993–94 prices

Notes: Service sectors include trade and hotels, transport and communication, financial and business services, and social and personal services.

Source: Government of India, *National Accounts Statistics* (various issues).

of the whole sector at 1993–94 prices rose from Rs1,735 billion in 1991–92 to Rs2,630 billion in 1995–96 and gradually declined to Rs2,327 billion in 2002–03.

Table 5.1 compares growth rates of GDP between 1981–82 and 1990–91 and those between 1991–92 and 2003–04. Growth rates of gross value added accelerated in two sectors: trade and hotels and transport and communication after economic reforms. They decelerated in three sectors: mining, electricity, gas and water supply, and financial and business services. Although the acceleration is not significant, GDP growth rates improved slightly after economic reforms. For four service sectors – trade and hotels, transport and communication, financial and business services, and social and personal services – growth rates were higher than 7 per cent after 1991–92. Their relative contributions to growth of GDP between 1995–96 and 2003–04 were 18.5 per cent, 14.9 per cent, 15.2 per cent and 15.5 per cent respectively.

Table 5.1 Growth rates of gross domestic product between 1981–82 and 1990–91 and between 1991–92 and 2003–04 (%)

Industries	*1981–82 to 1990–91*	*1991–92 to 2003–04*
Agriculture	3.0	2.5
Mining	7.2	4.4*
Manufacturing	7.2	6.5
Electricity, gas and water supply	8.9	5.3*
Construction	4.3	5.7
Trade and hotels	5.8	7.9*
Transport and communications	5.7	9.3*
Financial and business services	9.6	7.5*
Social and personal services	6.4	7.1
GDP	5.4	5.9

Note: *Acceleration and deceleration after 1991 was significant at the 1% level. In investigating the issue of whether there was acceleration or deceleration in the growth rate of gross value added after economic reforms, dummy variables were used to allow both the intercept and the slope to be different after 1991–92. Thus, we estimate a typical regression equation:

$$\ln Y = \alpha + \alpha' D + \beta t + \beta' Dt$$

where α is a dummy variable with values equal to zero for the years up to 1990–91 and 1 thereafter. The coefficient of the multiplicative dummy term, β', if it is positive or negative and significant, shows that there was acceleration or deceleration in the gross rate in the post-economic reform period.

Source: See Figure 5.1.

IT and IT enabled services (ITES) industries developed rapidly after the economic reforms. The Indian IT-ITES industries are broadly categorized into IT services, ITES-BPO, engineering services and R&D, software products and hardware segments. IT services have risen as a result of outsourcing from companies in developed countries, and the development of telecommunications has made it possible to outsource software development. Business process outsourcing (BPO) means outsourcing of some of the non-critical and non-core areas, covering a variety of low-end to high-end services claims processing and call-centre operations in insurance, loan processing, billing and operations in telecommunications, and research and development in pharmaceuticals and auto and auto-component industries. Many companies in developed countries have started to take advantage of outsourcing of IT and ITES to restructure their businesses and reduce operational costs. As a result, Indian IT and ITES industries have grown rapidly, using human resources with English-speaking and skilled manpower. Revenues from IT and ITES industries increased rapidly from US$5 billion in 1999–2000 to US$36 billion in 2005–06. However, the influence of IT and ITES industries on GDP is still limited; their share in GDP was only 4.8 per cent in 2005–06 (NASSCOM, 2006). IT and ITES industries depend on exports, and in 2005–06 exports accounted for 62.3 per cent of the total revenue. On the other hand, other service industries depend on the domestic market, and the growth of the service sector is related to domestic factors.

There are four reasons that the service sector has grown rapidly after economic reforms. First, globalization of the economy has promoted not only foreign trade but also a physical redistribution of the domestic market. Trade and road transport have developed to meet growing demand, and increased national incomes have encouraged consumption of services. Second, the progress of urbanization has created new services to meet consumption in urban areas. Third, the rise in living standards has led to the growth of expenditure on services including education and medical and health services. Fourth, the liberalization of regulation on the service sector has led to an expansion of business opportunities. Telephone box and mobile phone networks have been spreading, and banking has grown to meet the demands of a rising middle class.

On the other hand, growth rates for the agriculture and manufacturing sectors dropped after the 1990s although the deceleration was insignificant. Figure 5.2 shows industry-wise growth rates after 1991–92,

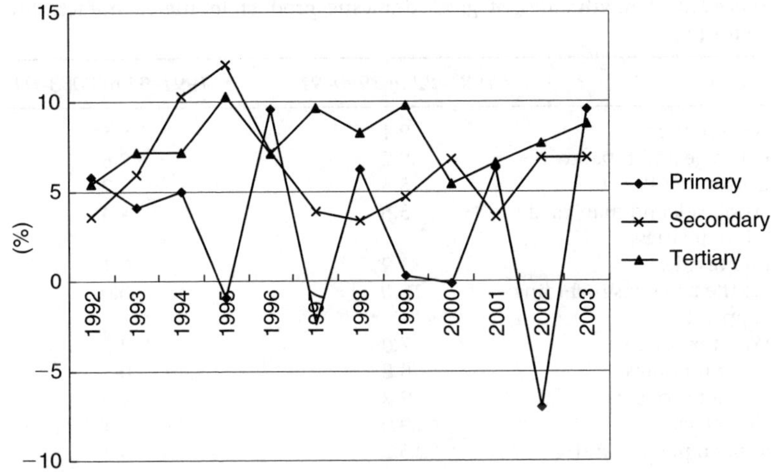

Figure 5.2 Industry-wise growth rates
Source: See Figure 5.1.

and GDP growth rates can be seen to have fluctuated depending on the performance of agriculture. The correlation coefficient between GDP growth rates and primary industry growth rates was 0.71, while that between GDP growth rates and tertiary industry growth rates was 0.32. Although the primary sector accounted for only 24.0 per cent in 2001–02, 72.2 per cent of the population lived in rural area (Census of India, 2001).[2] The influence of agricultural production on GDP is large. As the share of irrigated area is low, crops depend on rainfall during the monsoon season. Rainfall was much lower than normal in 1995–96, 1997–98, 2000–01 and 2002–03, and in these years except 1999–2000 growth of agricultural production was negative; GDP growth rates were 7.3 per cent, 4.8 per cent, 4.4 per cent and 4.0 per cent respectively.

The manufacturing sector stagnated between 1997–98 and 2001–02; the investment boom during the mid-1990s had not led to rapid growth. During the 1990s the organized sector accounted for two-thirds of domestic product in the manufacturing sector, and Table 5.2 compares growth rates of domestic product in the sector between 1981–82 and 1990–91 and between 1991–92 and 2003–04. In the 1980s, export-oriented industries such as apparel and leather goods had grown rapidly by more than 9 per cent under the background of a gradual rupee depreciation. Production of petroleum products and cement had risen

Table 5.2 Growth rates of gross domestic product in the manufacturing sector (%)

	1981–82 to 1990–91	*1991–92 to 2003–04*
Food products	9.1	5.5*
Beverage and tobacco	8.2	9.8
Cotton textiles	5.5	2.2
Wool, silk and man-made fibre textiles	5.6	4.4
Jute textiles	1.9	1.1
Textile products including apparel	12.0	10.0
Wood products	7.0	2.7
Paper products	8.8	0.5*
Leather products	9.3	4.0
Chemicals	9.0	8.1
Rubber, plastics and petroleum	16.2	5.7*
Non-metallic products	11.1	6.2*
Basic metal products	5.2	6.5
Metal products	6.2	7.6
Machinery	5.8	5.4
Electrical machinery	10.2	7.8
Transport equipment	5.2	7.6
All	7.9	6.7

Note: *Acceleration and deceleration after 1991 was significant at the 1% level. The method of calculation is same as for Table 5.1.
Source: See Figure 5.1.

to meet growing demand, and growth rates of rubber, plastics and petroleum and non-metallic product industries were 16.2 per cent and 11.1 per cent respectively.

Growth rates of the manufacturing sector fell from 7.9 per cent during the 1980s to 6.7 per cent after 1991–92. Before the economic reforms, it was argued that government regulations had distorted the market mechanism and made import-substitution industries profitable (Bhagwati and Srinivasan, 1975). In this view, investment should have shifted from import-substitution industries to export industries after deregulation and trade reforms, but growth rates of apparel and leather industries went down. As export industries face severe competition in international markets, it is difficult to maintain growth rates, and it is such external factors that have prevented rapid growth of these industries.

Growth rates for the petroleum products industry (mainly refineries) declined because of an increase of imports. As net imports of petroleum products rose from 7.6 million tonnes in 1992–93 to 23.1 million tonnes in 1998–99, the share of domestic production in gross availability declined from 86.9 per cent to 73.7 per cent during the period. Competition with imports decreased domestic production of the petroleum industry by the end of the 1990s, and as a result the growth rates of rubber, plastics and petroleum industries decelerated significantly in the post-reform period. As mentioned later, however, the industry recovered and started growing after 1999.

The main non-metallic product industry is the cement industry. After liberalization competition became tough, and during the three years 1997–99 the real prices of cement maintained the same level or went down because of stagnation of the national economy and competition among companies; the profitability of small firms deteriorated (Vaidya, 2002).

Growth rates significantly improved in four industries – beverage and tobacco, basic metal products, metal products, and transport equipment. These four industries mainly depend on the domestic market, and as the domestic market has expanded constantly and competition in the international market is tough, the structure of the manufacturing sector has not shifted from an import-substitution orientation. The composition of exports did not change much between 1996–97 and 2003–04. The share of jewellery and apparel in total exports was 27.7 per cent in 1996–97 and 29.2 per cent in 2003–04, and these two goods are still main items for export. The influence of imports and exports on the manufacturing sector increased from the mid-1990s onwards; petroleum products are an example.

There are two reasons why the investment boom only lasted for a short time. First, sales did not grow as much as expected; as production capacity grew faster than demand, overcapacity developed and utilization rates declined (Uchikawa, 2001). Although India has a population of more than 1 billion, the domestic market is narrow compared with the population. Second, high interest rates above 10 per cent became a burden; for example in April 1997 the prime lending rate over Rs200,000 ranged between 14.0 per cent and 14.5 per cent. As long as sales are rising payment of interest is not a problem, but when sales start to decline interest payments oppress profits.

The progress of globalization forced India to open her economy. With globalization of the economy, urbanization, a rise of living standard and liberalization stimulated the service sector. Although economic reforms did not accelerate growth rates of the manufacturing sector, each industry adjusted itself to globalization.

Benefits of globalization: IT and the petroleum sector

After economic reforms, India's trade direction has changed, as illustrated by Table 5.3 which shows India's regional trade. Imports from ASEAN and North-east Asia, that is China, South Korea, Taiwan and Japan and so on, increased between 1996–97 and 2004–05 from a share of 7.5–8.1 per cent (ASEAN) of India's total imports and from 11.8–14.8 per cent (North-east Asia) respectively during the period. On the other

Table 5.3 India's regional trade (US$ millions)

	1996–97		*2000–01*		*2004–05*	
Imports						
EU countries	10,523	(26.9)	10,640	(21.1)	18,716	(17.1)
Africa	2,292	(5.9)	1,613	(3.2)	3,299	(3.0)
North America	3,930	(10.0)	3,412	(6.8)	7,594	(7.0)
ASEAN	2,934	(7.5)	4,147	(8.2)	8,864	(8.1)
North-east Asia	4,603	(11.8)	5,618	(11.1)	16,115	(14.8)
Others	10,461	(26.7)	9,423	(18.6)	24,210	(22.2)
Unspecified	4,389	(11.2)	15,683	(31.0)	30,376	(27.8)
India's total imports	39,132	(100)	50,536	(100)	109,173	(100)
Exports						
EU countries	8,844	(26.4)	10,670	(23.9)	18,118	(21.7)
Africa	1,345	(4.0)	1,822	(4.1)	4,218	(5.0)
North America	6,908	(20.6)	9,962	(22.4)	14,633	(17.5)
ASEAN	2,902	(8.7)	2,914	(6.5)	8,426	(10.1)
North-east Asia	5,458	(16.3)	6,282	(14.1)	13,223	(15.8)
Others	7,516	(22.5)	11,020	(24.7)	24,509	(29.3)
Unspecified	496	(1.5)	1,890	(4.2)	409	(0.5)
India's total exports	33,470	(100)	44,560	(100)	83,536	(100)

Note: Figures in parenthesis are percentages.
Source: Government of India, Export Import Data Bank (http://commerce.nic.in/eidb/default.asp).

hand, the share of imports from the EU and North America declined although the amounts of import rose from US$10,523 million to US$18,716 million, and from US$3,930 million to US$7,594 million respectively. This means that India's economic relations with North-east Asia and South-east Asia have strengthened. India is importing mainly electrical machinery and machinery from North-east Asia; the two items accounted for 41.2 per cent of total imports from the area in 2004–05. FDI from Japan and Korea has also induced imports from those countries; units of Japanese and Korean companies in India procure capital goods and crucial components from their related companies in Japan and Korea, and some components from their related units in ASEAN. India is importing mainly edible oil, machinery and electrical machinery from ASEAN; the three items accounted for 47.7 per cent of total imports from the area in 2004–05. On the other hand, India imposes high customs tariffs on palm oil from Malaysia and Indonesia, which has created trade conflicts between India and those countries. As we shall discuss later, India must maintain high rates of customs tariffs to protect small farmers, although domestic production of edible oil is not sufficient.

Intra firm trade has developed not only between India and North-east Asia but also between India and ASEAN. While the share of exports to ASEAN in India's total exports rose from 8.7 per cent to 10.1 per cent between 1996–97 and 2004–05, that to North-east Asia fell from 16.3 per cent to 15.8 per cent due to a decrease of exports to Japan from US$2,188 million to US$2,128 million. India exports mainly iron ore, jewellery, and iron and steel to North-east Asia; the three items accounted for 57.9 per cent in total exports to the area in 2004–05. The construction boom in China has caused a rapid increase of imports of iron and steel from India. India is exporting mainly petroleum products, jewellery and organic chemicals to ASEAN; the three items accounted for 44.4 per cent in total exports to the area in 2004–05. Although India is exporting machinery and electrical machinery to ASEAN, their share was only 5.2 per cent and 2.7 per cent respectively. Units of Japanese and Korean companies in India are not active for exports to their related units in ASEAN.

While foreign direct investment clearly rose after the economic reforms, most of the foreign manufacturing companies that invested in India did so mainly to catch the domestic market. India has not become an export base for multinational companies. This is in sharp contrast with China, where multinational companies have invested to set up a manufacturing exports base. In fact, exports by foreign companies accounted for more than half of total exports in the 2000s. There are two reasons that multinational companies have hesitated to set up export bases in India. First, India's manufacturing sector has faced labour problems; compared with other countries labour laws are strict in India. For example, the Industrial Disputes Act (1947) prohibits lay-offs, retrenchment and closure by industrial units employing not less than 100 workers without prior permission of the government. The ILO argues that the employment security regulation has induced employers to keep establishment sizes artificially small, particularly sacrificing economies of scale (ILO, 1996). However, units employing 100 to 199 raised their share of their employment in total employment of the organized manufacturing sector along with units employing 50 to 99 between 1979–80 and 1997–98. Medium-scale units were a dynamic sector in employment and investment (Uchikawa, 2003). The real problem is not labour laws but politics; local politics have been involved in business, and labour laws have many loopholes. Second, conditions of infrastructure such as power, the transportation network and water supply are inadequate to run factories without problems.

After economic reforms, service exports became important. As mentioned earlier, the progress of globalization forced companies in developed countries to have recourse to outsourcing, and IT-ITES industries in particular have developed in India. Exports of IT services and software increased from US$1.1 billion in 1996–97 to US$9.2 billion in 2003–04, while exports of ITES-BPO rose from US$0.6 billion in 1999–2000 to US$3.6 billion in 2003–04. Many multinational companies have set up software development centres and captive units in India. IT and ITES industries are free from labour disputes, and employees with skills can move to other companies easily if they are not satisfied with their present employment conditions; however job-hopping is a serious problem in these industries.

Among developing countries, India has sustained leadership over other competing outsourcing destinations. There are three reasons. First, India has a skilled workforce; the Indian education system places a strong emphasis on mathematics and science, resulting in a large number of science and engineering graduates. Mastery over quantitative concepts coupled with English proficiency has resulted in a skill-set that has enabled the country to take advantage of the current international demand for IT. Second, a market-oriented training has strengthened competitiveness of Indian IT companies. As technology in the IT industry is developing fast, retraining of employees is inevitable and leading Indian companies conduct research and identify future technology needs and gaps in skills and make necessary arrangements to train their workforce. Third, Indian companies are in the forefront of obtaining various quality certifications like the Software Engineering Institute–Capability Maturity Model (SEI-CMM) in the software area, and the Customer Operations Performance Centre (COPC) in the BPO area. Quality certifications have become essential for relatively new and emerging Indian service providers to show their potential customers that they are capable of delivering quality services. Besides, obtaining early certifications is used as a differentiator in competition and a tool in marketing. Western companies especially from the USA have used CMM certification as one of the criteria in choice of vendor (Munirathnam, 2005).

Development of IT and ITES industries has improved the balance of payments (Table 5.4). IT companies often send their employees abroad to implement on-site jobs, and these employees send their salaries to India. Besides, many IT engineers have settled down in the USA. As software business has developed, private transfers have increased. On the other hand, GDP growth has encouraged imports. Although exports have grown, the trade balance has expanded due to an increase of imports.

Table 5.4 India's balance of payments (US$ millions)

	1999–00	*2000–01*	*2001–02*	*2002–03*	*2003–04*	*2004–05*
1 Trade balance (a+b)	−14,370	−12,703	−11,574	−10,690	−15,454	−38,130
(a) Exports	44,894	44,915	44,703	53,774	64,723	80,831
(b) Imports	59,264	57,618	56,277	64,464	80,177	118,961
2 Invisibles, net (c+d+e)	10,780	13,485	14,974	17,035	26,015	31,699
(c) Services of	2,478	4,577	3,324	3,643	6,591	14,630
which Software*	5,750	6,884	6,884	8,863	11,750	16,626
(d) Transfers of	13,134	12,509	15,856	16,838	23,396	21,048
which private	12,798	12,125	15,398	16,387	22,833	20,459
(e) Income	−4,832	−3,601	−4,206	−3,446	−3,972	−3,979
Current Account (1+2)	−3,590	782	3,400	6,345	10,561	−6,431

Notes: *This figure is not the same as the export amount announced by NASSCOM.
Source: Reserve Bank of India, *RBI Bulletin* (various issues).

Since the level of net invisible earnings increased because of the growth of service exports and private transfers, the current account changed from deficit to surplus from 2000–01. In 2004–05 the boom of the national economy caused a jump of imports and the current account fell into deficit again. Foreign exchange reserves have accumulated from US$33,422 million in June 1999 to US$138,370 million in June 2005. IT and ITES industries have developed, taking advantage of off-shore service business, and the balance of payments improved in the 2000s. India is an example that developing countries can enjoy the benefits of globalization.

There is another reason that forces India to adjust herself to globalization. Economic development has increased energy consumption since the mid-1990s, and the 2000s petroleum accounted for around 27 per cent of India's imports. India became the 6th largest consumer of crude oil in the world in 2003, from 10th in 1997 (Table 5.5). In 1997 the exploration and refinery sectors were opened to the private sector and foreign companies in order to promote new exploration of oil and gas fields. Development of gas fields increased production of natural gas from 18,335 million cubic metres in 1993–94 to 31,962 million cubic metres in 2003–04. On the other hand, while domestic production of crude oil has not risen, India's imports of crude oil rose from 34.39 million tonnes in 1999–2000 to 81.99 million tonnes in 2003–04 (Figure 5.3).

Such circumstances have led the Government of India to take action in its foreign policy to acquire overseas assets. For example, ONGC (Oil and Natural Gas Corporation), which is a leading National

Table 5.5 Estimates of consumption of crude oil (million tonnes)

	1997	*1998*	*1999*	*2000*	*2001*	*2002*	*2003*
USA	848.0	863.8	888.9	897.6	896.1	897.4	914.3
China	185.6	190.3	207.2	230.1	232.2	246.9	275.2
Japan	265.0	253.6	257.3	255.5	247.5	243.6	248.7
Germany	136.5	136.6	132.4	129.8	131.6	127.4	125.1
Russian Federation	129.1	123.7	126.2	123.5	122.3	123.5	124.7
India	83.3	92.5	100.3	106.1	107.0	111.3	113.3
Total World	3,395.2	3,416.9	3,485.1	3,526.1	3,538.2	3,562.6	3,636.6

Source: Government of India, *Energy Statistics 2003–04*, p. 46.

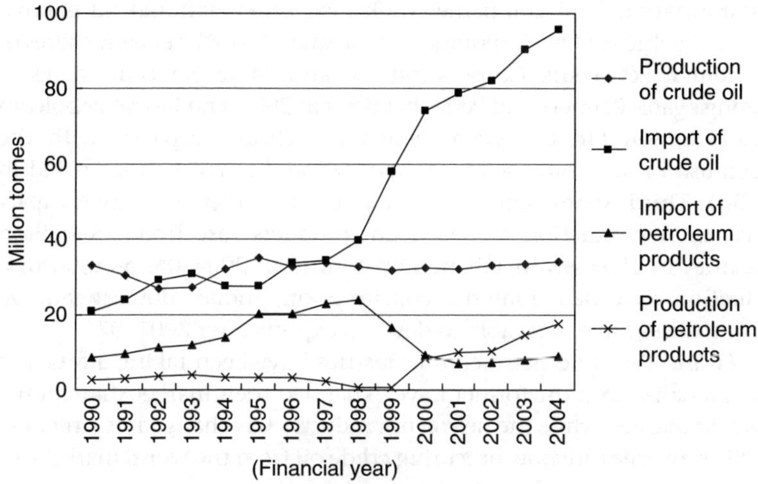

Figure 5.3 Production and imports of crude oil
Source: Government of India, *Annual Report of Ministry of Petroleum and Natural Gas* (various issues).

Oil Company, set up a wholly owned subsidiary ONGC Videsh Limited (OVL). The government provides OVL a single window clearance for overseas upstream projects irrespective of investments involved. OVL has 14 overseas assets of oil and gas fields in 14 countries: Myanmar, Russia, Vietnam, Iran, Iraq, Syria, Libya, Sudan, Nigeria, Egypt, Qatar, Cuba, Columbia and Brazil. Without such a global approach, India cannot meet its expanding demand for energy.

Liberalization has changed the industrial structure of the petroleum sector. For example, a private company, Reliance, set up a refinery capable of processing 27 million metric tonnes per annum and started production in 1999. India now has 18 refineries, and among them 17 are run by the public sector, and 16 have an annual capacity below 10 million tonnes. Nationalized oil companies have been forced to adjust themselves to liberalization from the 2000s. First, upstream and downstream integration has progressed; in 2002, ONGC diversified into the downstream sector, taking over Mangalore Refinery and Petrochemicals Ltd from the A V Birla Group, and is set to enter into retailing. On the other hand, Hindustan Petroleum Corporation Ltd, which is the second largest refining and marketing company, has entered into exploration and development. Second, some national oil companies took over other national oil companies: the Indian Oil Corporation Ltd acquired 51.81 per cent shares of Chennai Petroleum Corporation Ltd and 74.46 per cent shares of Bongaigaon Refinery and Petrochemicals in 2001; and Bharat Petroleum Corporation Ltd has strengthened its refining capacity with the acquisition of Numaligarh Refinery Ltd and Kochi Refineries Ltd in 2001. Third, state-owned oil companies have expanded their capacity: total production of petroleum products rose from 55 million tonnes in 1995–96 to 118 million tonnes in 2004–05. As total production exceeded domestic consumption, Indian downstream oil companies have been able to develop exports after 2001–02.

IT and ITES and petroleum industries have been taking advantage of globalization; the former have expanded their market share in the world market, while the petroleum industry has changed its structure. Oil companies are now procuring crude oil from the world market and exporting products back to the world market.

Economic growth and poverty reduction

India maintained stable economic growth in the 1980s and 1990s, during which time the ratio of population below the poverty line in the total population declined between 1983 and 1999. The poverty line is based on the rupee value of a specified nutritional requirement, and it is stipulated by the Planning Commission that the calorie standard for a typical individual in rural areas is 2,400 calories per capita per day and 2,100 calories in urban areas. The cost of grains to fulfil this normative standard is calculated, and that cost is the poverty line. The poverty ratio of combined rural and urban areas decreased from 54.9 per cent in 1973 to 26.1 per cent in 1999 (Figure 5.4), when annual GDP growth rates were 3.9 per cent between 1973 and 1983 and 5.6 per cent between 1983 and 1999. The rate of decrease remained steady after 1983.

There are several factors to promote poverty alleviation and four in particular: improvement of productivity in agriculture; improvement of incomes of farmers and agricultural labourers; relatively stable prices; and a public distribution system to distribute food for the poor at low prices.

First, improvement of land productivity has made it possible to supply foodstuffs at stable prices without depending on imports. India's population rose from 361 million in 1951 to 1,012 million in 2001, and

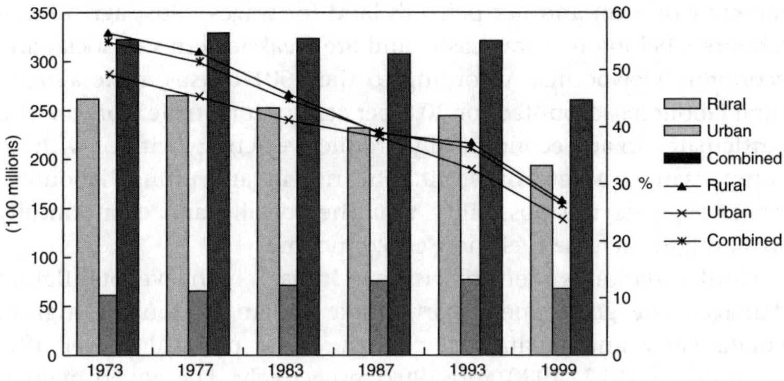

Figure 5.4 Population below the poverty line and its share in total population
Source: Government of India, *Report of the National Commission on Labour*, p.56.

unless the increase of per capita production of food grains keeps up with the population growth, food grains may become in short supply. Production of food grains increased from 48 million tonnes to 171 million tonnes during the same period. The use of high-yield varieties of wheat started to spread in the Punjab and Haryana after the mid-1960s, and the green revolution has dramatically changed traditional unstable planting with low productivity and succeeded in increasing food production, mainly wheat. However, impacts have been limited in terms of regions and variety. In the 1980s, high-yield varieties of rice, maize, pulses, oil seeds, cotton and sugarcane spread and their production increased. Moreover, the green revolution has reached eastern states like Bihar and Orissa where agriculture was backward, and as a result the per capita production of food grains had grown up to 1991.

Second, farmers' incomes and wages of agricultural labourers have risen due to improvements in productivity. In the regions where the green revolution has diffused, poverty clearly declined. Even during the low-growth period between 1973 and 1983, poverty alleviation in specific regions helped to reduce the poverty ratio all over India. As the social structure is varied from region to region, generalization is difficult, but it can be stated that there is a hierarchy of land owners followed by self-employed farmers, tenants, and agricultural labourers. An agricultural labourer is defined by census as a person who works on another person's land for wages in money or some kind of share. He has no right of lease or contract on the land on which he works and merely works on another person's land for wages. Most agricultural labourers belong to a low caste, and are weak in terms of social and economic viewpoints. According to the 2001 census, male agricultural labourers accounted for 20.8 per cent of total male workers who participated in any economically productive activity with or without compensation, wages or profit. The rise in agricultural labourers' wages suggests the possibility that the socially and economically weak might increase their household income.

Third, inflation is a sensitive issue in India. A high level of inflation damaged the government parties like Indian National Congress, Janata Party and Janata Dal and they lost political power after elections in 1977, 1980 and 1991 respectively. The government is keen to maintain prices at a stable level, so that as agricultural labourers purchase food grains from the market, the stability of prices contributes to improvements of purchasing power.

Fourth, India has a public distribution system under which states' governments procure rice and wheat from farmers at specific prices and distributes them to poor families at lower prices. The food subsidies for the public distribution system are a burden on the government budget, but although their inefficiency is criticized they have contributed to the food security of families under the poverty line.

The poverty ratio declined dramatically between 1973 and 1999, but the population below the poverty line was still 260 million even in 1999. It was pointed out widely, moreover, that the figure in 1999 was underestimated due to changes in the sampling method in the national sample surveys. By comparison, the population below the poverty line had fluctuated around 320 million between 1973 and 1993. Three factors are relevant: the increase of the population, a shrinkage of the average size of operational land holdings, and the slow growth of employment opportunities, all prevent poverty alleviation.

The first fact as, growth of the population, increased the population below the poverty line. There was a slight decline in population growth from 2.0 per cent between 1983 and 1993 to 1.9 per cent between 1993 and 1999, but the constant increase of population has made poverty alleviation difficult.

Secondly, the increase of population reduced the average size of operational land holdings; the share of households working two hectares went down from 27.4 per cent in 1976 to 22.0 per cent in 1990. The shrinkage of operational land holdings leads to a reduction of income unless improvements of land productivity compensate for it. In backward areas with inadequate irrigation systems, high yield varieties which need larger amounts of water and fertilizer have not spread yet. The marginalization of land holdings therefore reduces farmers' incomes.

Third, the growth of employment has been unable to keep up with that of the labour force, and unemployment and underemployment lead to instability of income. Despite the fall in growth of population, the growth of population in the working-age group (above 15 years old) has continued to accelerate. However, the growth of labour force decelerated from 2.43 per cent between 1983 and 1994 to 1.31 per cent between 1994 and 1999, and a substantial part of the population in the working-age group has withdrawn from the labour force. While a part of the decline in the labour force can be explained by an increase in attendance at educational institutions, some of those in the working-age group have withdrawn from labour force due to non-availability of work (Government of India, 2002b). On the other hand, growth of the workforce, that is employment on a current daily basis slowed from 2.7 per cent between 1983 and 1994 to 1.07 per cent between 1994 and 1999 (Table 5.6). As underemployment is serious in India, the current daily basis is a better measure to express unemployment, under which, the activity status of a person for each of the preceding seven days is recorded. A person who worked for at least one hour but less than four hours is considered having worked for half-a-day; for four hours or more the person is considered employed for the whole day (Govt. of Tamil Nadu, 2000). Employment growth decelerated in both rural and urban areas between 1994 and 1999, but particularly in rural areas it grew by only 0.67 per cent between 1993 and 1999. As a result, the unemployment ratio rose from 5.99 per cent in 1993 to 7.32 per cent in 1999.

As non-availability of work made some of the working-age group withdraw from the labour force, the situation was more serious. Many reports bring out a common message that 'if the experiences of the late nineties are extrapolated i.e., repeated in future, then India is going to face increasingly higher incidence of unemployment, with an ever increasing gap between the demand for jobs and supply of job opportunities' (Government of India, 2002a).

Since economic growth improved slightly in the 1990s, the deceleration of employment growth implies a decline of employment elasticity.

Table 5.6 Employment and unemployment (millions)

				Growth rates (%)	
	1983	*1993*	*1999*	*1983 to 1993*	*1993 to 1999*
All India					
Workforce	239.57	315.84	336.75	2.70	1.07
No. of unemployed	21.76	20.13	26.58	−0.08	4.74
Labour force	261.33	335.97	363.33	2.43	1.31
Unemployment rate	(8.33)	(5.99)	(7.32)		
Rural					
Workforce	187.92	241.04	250.89	2.40	0.67
No. of unemployed	16.26	14.34	19.50	−1.19	5.26
Labour force	204.18	255.38	270.39	2.15	0.96
Unemployment rate	(7.96)	(5.62)	(7.21)		
Urban					
Workforce	51.64	74.80	85.84	3.59	2.32
No. of unemployed	5.51	5.80	7.11	0.49	3.45
Labour force	57.15	80.60	92.95	3.33	2.40
Unemployment rate	(9.64)	(7.20)	(7.65)		

Note: All estimates are on a current daily basis measure. Figures in parentheses indicate percentages.
Source: Government of India, *Tenth Five Year Plan*, p. 159.

Table 5.7 shows that employment elasticity across all industries decreased from 0.52 between 1983 and 1993 to 0.16 between 1993 and 2000. Particularly in agriculture it decreased from 0.7 to 0.01 over the period. As agriculture accounted for 61.7 per cent of total employment in 1999, its impact on all industries was large. In agriculture, mechanization has progressed, but although it has increased productivity it did not contribute to growth of employment.

During the 1980s, the public sector had an oversupply of manpower. After the economic reforms, surplus labour was retrenched through voluntary retirement schemes which encouraged retirement of employees by offers of lump-sum payments. Employment decreased in mining, electricity, gas and water supply, and social services between

Table 5.7 Employment elasticity across industries

Industries	*1983–93*	*1993–2000*
Agriculture	0.70	0.01
Mining	0.59	–0.41
Manufacturing	0.38	0.33
Electricity, gas and water supply	0.63	−0.52
Construction	0.86	0.82
Trade and hotels	0.68	0.62
Transport and communication	0.55	0.63
Financial and business services	0.45	0.64
Social and personal services	0.68	−0.25
All	0.52	0.16

Source: Government of India, *Tenth Five Year Plan*, p. 160.

1993 and 2000, reflected in the negative employment elasticity in the industries.

The number of workers in the organized manufacturing sector clearly decreased after 1997. As noted earlier, the organized sector is defined as factories employing 10 or more workers using power and those employing 20 or more workers without using power. Although the number of workers in the organized manufacturing sector increased from 6.2 million in 1991–92 to 7.6 million in 1997–98, it decreased to 6.1 million in 2002–03, for three reasons in particular. First, as the investment boom was over and capacity underutilization made its appearance, factories reduced their workforce; second, competition forced companies to retrench redundant workers through the voluntary retirement schemes; and third, many textile factories closed down after 1985.

On the other hand, employment elasticity rose in the transport and communication and the financial and business services industries. In transport and communication, employment increased from 9.88 million in 1993 to 13.65 million in 1999, by 5.5 per cent per annum. Development of the industry absorbed a significant part of the labour force in the 1990s, due to its labour intensive nature; growth of employment and gross value added accelerated between 1993 and 1999. Conversely, the growth of gross value added decelerated between 1993 and 1999 in financial and business services where, as a result, employment elasticity increased.

The regional gap widened after the economic reforms, and the fact that advanced states succeeded in reducing the poverty ratio suggests there is an efficient way to do so. To this end I analyse the relationship between per capita net state domestic product (NSDP) and poverty. Goa had the highest per capita NSDP at 1993–94 prices in 1993–94, and Punjab, Maharashtra, Haryana and Gujarat followed (Table 5.8). Bihar had the lowest per capita NSDP at 1993–94 prices in 1993, followed by Orissa and Uttar Pradesh. Goa produces iron ore and Punjab and Haryana are agriculturally developed states. Maharashtra and Gujarat are industrial and commercially developed states. In large areas of backward states, that is Bihar, Orissa and Uttar Pradesh, irrigation has not spread and agriculture depends on rainfall. Although the green revolution has reached eastern states such as Bihar and Orissa, the share of irrigated area in farmlands is still lower than in other states. Differences in agricultural productivity caused the regional gap of NSDP between states (Hirashima, 2003). In 2001 the share of irrigated area in the total area cultivating food grains was 96.6 per cent in Punjab, 85.0 per cent in Haryana, 49.5 per cent in Bihar, and 30.4 per cent in Orissa. The ranking of per capita NSDP did not change between 1993–94 and 2001–02: the order was Goa, Punjab, Maharashtra, Haryana and Gujarat from the top; and Bihar, Uttar Pradesh, Assam and Orissa from the bottom in 2001–02. While per capita NSDP of Goa was 5.5 times higher than that of Bihar in 1993–94, the gap between Goa and Bihar became 8.0 times in 2001–02.

In the states where per capita NSDP is high, the poverty ratio is clearly declining. In the states where per capita NSDP is above the average of all India except Punjab, the poverty ratio declined by more than 10 percentage points between 1993–94 and 1999–2000. In Maharashtra the poverty ratio was 25 per cent in 1999–2000; although it is a business centre including Mumbai and the industrially developed area, the regional gap within the state is wide because it has a dry area up on the Deccan Plateau. On the other hand, in the states where per capita NSDP is below the average of all India except Rajasthan and Bihar, the poverty ratio declined by less than 10 percentage points between 1993–94 and 1999–2000. In spite of the decline of the poverty ratio by 12.4 per cent point during the period, the ratio in Bihar was 42.6 per cent in 1999–2000.

The states where per capita NSDP is above the average of all India have reduced poverty more efficiently than the states where per capita

Table 5.8 Per capita NSDP and the poverty ratio

Financial year	*Per capita NSDP at 1993–94 prices (Rs) 2001–02*	*Growth rates of per capita NSDP (%) 1993–94 to 2001–02*	*Poverty ratio (%)*		*Population growth rates (%) 1991 to 2001*
			1993–94	*1999–2000*	
Goa	28,304	7.3	14.9	4.4	1.4
Punjab	15,255	2.5	11.8	6.2	1.8
Maharashtra	14,892	2.7	36.9	25.0	2.1
Haryana	14,250	3.1	25.1	8.7	2.5
Gujarat	13,684	3.3	24.2	14.1	2.0
Tamil Nadu	13,108	4.6	35.0	21.1	1.3
Karnataka	11,516	5.6	33.2	20.0	1.6
Himachal Pradesh	11,402	4.7	28.4	7.6	1.6
Kerala	11,046	3.9	25.4	12.7	0.9
Average of All India	10,774	4.2	36.0	26.1	2.0
Andhra Pradesh	10,590	4.4	22.2	15.8	1.3
West Bengal	10,375	5.4	35.7	27.0	1.7
Tripura	10,255	8.3	39.0	34.4	1.5
Meghalaya	9,514	4.5	37.9	33.9	2.7
Arunachal Pradesh	9,413	1.0	39.4	33.5	2.3
Rajasthan	8,819	3.8	27.4	15.3	2.5
Madhya Pradesh	7,699	2.2	42.5	37.4	−0.9
Manipur	6,715	2.7	33.8	28.5	2.7
Orissa	6,105	2.6	48.6	47.2	1.5
Assam	6,059	0.5	40.9	36.1	1.7
Uttar Pradesh	5,885	1.6	40.9	31.2	1.8
Bihar	3,554	2.4	55.0	42.6	−0.4

Source: Central Statistical Organization Homepage (http://mospi.nic.in/cso.htm) Planning Commission, *National Human Development Report 2001*.

NSDP is below the average. To promote poverty alleviation all over India, per capita growth rates in backward states should be raised.

There are three conditions to reduce poverty. First, it is necessary to enrich institutions that provide a safety network. Households with poor assets and without land are vulnerable to income shocks due to drought and so on, and face great difficulty in recovering their incomes to levels before the shocks. Therefore, public investment projects, such as afforestation and construction of irrigation canals and roads in areas prone to natural disasters like drought, may prevent agricultural labourers' incomes falling below the poverty line to some extent. Maharashtra has implemented the employment guarantee scheme, which provides the poor with a method of overcoming crisis through employment (Kurosaki and Yamazaki, 2002). The government must also protect small farmers from fluctuations in international prices of agricultural products.

Second, an increase of investment for irrigation is necessary to improve agricultural productivity. A state-wide analysis shows that the poverty ratio is low in agriculturally developed states, which have good irrigation systems. Public investment to construct irrigation canals compensates for private investment to dig irrigation wells. They do not substitute another. In some areas, the digging of too many wells has rapidly depleted levels of underground water, and random digging is also creating problems. Control of water resources is important in order to use them efficiently. Increased investment for irrigation is important from a medium term perspective.

Third, creation of non-farm employment is essential to alleviate poverty over the long-term. Because employment elasticity decreased, employment in rural areas has not increased significantly, and although public investment projects can absorb labour for short periods to rescue the poor, they are not sustainable due to budget restrictions. To increase non-farm employment there are three requirements: an increase in agricultural productivity to increase household incomes in the area; households then increase their expenditures and the retail and service sectors grow; the expansion of retail and service sectors then increases opportunities of non-farm employment.

As mentioned before, the high customs tariff on palm oil from Malaysia and Indonesia created trade conflict, but the government must maintain its stance to protect the weak if it is to win at election. If the government were seen to be sacrificing the weak to adjust to globalization, this would damage the government. Rural development is essential to improve the image of government, but more important is the goal that rural development leads to expansion of domestic demand. If growth of the domestic market decelerates, that may restrict economic growth in India.

Conclusion

The progress of globalization forced India to open her economy; India changed from an import-substitution strategy and started economic reforms. The reforms induced an investment boom in the manufacturing sector in the mid-1990s, but the boom did not last and the manufacturing sector stagnated between 1997–98 and 2001–02. Narrow domestic demand and high interest rates prevented growth of the manufacturing sector. On the other hand, the service sector has grown rapidly after economic reforms; improved physical distribution in the domestic market, urbanization and rising living standards promoted development of the service industry. Although economic reforms did not accelerate growth rates of the manufacturing sector, each industry has adjusted itself to globalization.

The IT, ITES and petroleum industries have been taking advantage of globalization. The IT and ITES industries expanded their market shares in the world market, and among developing countries India has sustained its leadership over other competing outsourcing destinations. Although the IT and ITES industries accounted for only 4.8 per cent of GDP in 2005–06, they have contributed to the balance of payments. Due to the growth of service exports and private transfers, the current account changed from deficit to surplus from 2000–01. Economic development has increased energy consumption since the mid-1990s, and India has started to actively procure energy resources from foreign countries. The petroleum industry has changed its structure; upstream and downstream integration has progressed. Some national oil companies have taken over other state-owned oil companies, and have expanded their capacity, and there has been the entry of a private company. Oil companies are procuring crude oil from the world market and exporting products to the world market. The IT, ITES and petroleum industries have been taking advantage of globalization.

The poverty ratio declined dramatically between 1973 and 1999. While the population below the poverty line declined between 1993 and 1999, it was still high at 260 million even in 1999. I have described factors that promote poverty alleviation: improvement of agricultural productivity, improvement of farmers' and agricultural labourers' incomes, relatively stable prices, and a public distribution system to distribute foods for the poor at low prices. On the other hand, increased population levels, the shrinkage of the average size of operational land holdings, and slow growth of employment opportunities all prevent poverty alleviation.

The regional gap has widened after economic reforms, with advanced states succeeding in reducing the poverty ratio. The states where per capita NSDP is above the average of all India have reduced poverty more efficiently than the states where per capita NSDP is below average. I suggest there are three conditions to reduce poverty: first, establishment of safety networks to prevent poverty from a short-term viewpoint; second, an increase in investment for irrigation to improve productivity of agriculture from a medium-term viewpoint; and third, creation of non-farm employment to alleviate poverty. Because employment elasticity decreased, employment in rural areas has not increased significantly.

India is enjoying the benefits of globalization. Although trickle-down effects of economic growth are pointed out, the benefits have not reached backward areas. Rural development is essential to reduce poverty. In India investment in agriculture and allied sectors has lagged behind other sectors. The share of agriculture and allied sectors in total gross capital formation decreased from 11.7 per cent in 1986–87 to 7.7 per cent in 2000–01. The government had to reduce the share of agriculture and allied sectors in total investment to restrict budget deficits, because globalization restricted government options and macroeconomic stability was preferred to investment in agriculture. However, such investment is essential for sustainable economic growth in India.

Notes

1 Banks are required to lend 40 per cent (32 per cent for foreign banks) of their advances towards the priority sector, which consists of the agricultural sector and small-scale industries.

2 The classification of an area as an urban unit in the Census of India is based on the following definition: (a) all places declared by the state government under a statute as a municipality, corporation, cantonment board or notified town-area committee, etc. (b) all other places which simultaneously satisfy or are expected to satisfy the following criteria: (1) a minimum population of 5,000; (2) at least 75 per cent of the male working population engaged in non-agricultural economic pursuits; and (3) a density of population of at least 400 per square kilometre (1,000 per square mile).

References

Bhagwati, J.N. and T.N. Srinivasan (1975) *Foreign Trade Regimes and Economic Development: India*. New York: National Bureau of Economic Research.

Chandrasekar, C.P. (1996) 'Explaining Post-reform Industrial Growth', *Economic and Political Weekly*, special issue.

Fujita, K. (2002) 'Indo Nogyoron, Gijyutsu, Policy, Structural Change' (in Japanese), in H. Esho, (ed.), *Gendai Minamiajia: Keizai Jiyuka no Yukue*. Tokyo: University of Tokyo Press.

Government of India (2001) Census of India, homepage, http://www.censusindia.net.

— (2002a) *Report of the Special Group on Targeting Ten Million Employment Opportunities per year over the Tenth Plan Period.*

— (2002b) *Tenth Five Years Plan.*

Government of Tamil Nadu (2000) *Tamil Nadu – An Economic Appraisal 1999–2000.*

Hirashima, S. (2003) 'Indo Nougyou no Chukitenbou to Nihon ODA', *Kosusaigaku Kennkyu*, March.

International Labour Organization (1996) *India: Economic Reforms and Labour Policies*. New Delhi: ILO.

Munirathnam, B. (2006) 'Indo no Jyohiogijyutsu Sangyo' (in Japanese), in S. Uchikawa (ed.), *Yakudosuru Indo Keizai*. Chiba, IDE–JETRO.

National Association of Software and Service Companies (NASSCOM) (2006) homepage, http://www.nasscom.org.

Kurosaki, T., and K. Yamazaki (2002) 'Minami Azia no Hinkonmondai to Nosonsetai Keizai' (in Japanese), in H. Esho (ed.), *Gendai Minamiajia: Keizai Jiyuka no Yukue*. Tokyo: University of Tokyo Press.

Uchikawa, S. (2001) 'Investment Boom and Underutilisation of Capacity in the 1990s', *Economic and Political Weekly*, 25 August.

— (2002) 'Investment Boom and Capital Goods Industry', in S. Uchikawa (ed.), *Economic Reforms and Industrial Structure in India*. Delhi: Manohar.

Vaidya, R.R. (2002) 'Intermediate Goods Industries: A Case Study of the Cement and Steel Industries', in S. Uchikawa (ed.), *Economic Reforms and Industrial Structure in India*. Delhi: Manohar.

6
India's Agricultural Challenges and their Implications for Growth of its Economy

Ramesh Chand

Agriculture continues to remain the predominant sector of the Indian economy even though its share in national output has declined from more than 50 per cent in the initial years after Independence from colonial rule in 1947 to less than 25 per cent in recent years. In terms of employment and livelihood, still around 58 per cent of workforce is engaged in agriculture as their principal occupation. Due to its importance in national output and employment, agriculture was paid special attention by India's policy-makers and development planners which helped this sector to play an important role in economic development of the country and in improving income and living standards of the vast population dependent on agriculture.

During the last decade and a half, several challenges have surfaced in Indian agriculture which are becoming more and more severe with the passage of time. These relate to growth of output, efficiency, equity and sustainability. There is widespread rural distress and frequent reports of farmers' committing suicide alleged to be caused by the dismal state of growth in farm output and farm incomes. Second, due to heavy share of agriculture in the national economy, this sector is becoming a drag on realizing a more than 7 per cent growth rate in the Indian economy. There is a danger that the Indian economy may not be able to sustain its high growth rate if performance of the agriculture sector does not improve. Against this backdrop this chapter highlights various challenges confronting India's agriculture sector and discusses the causes underlying these challenges. Suggestions for reforms in the agriculture sector are offered to overcome various challenges that afflict India's agriculture.

The biggest challenge is to reverse the sharp decline in the growth rate of the agriculture sector after the mid-1990s. The growth rate fell below the growth in the population dependent on agriculture implying that per capita income in agriculture is falling. This is considered a major factor for large-scale rural distress and the large number of suicidal deaths by farmers in various parts of the country.

The second biggest challenge is to ensure sustainable use of natural resources. While the need for accelerating agricultural growth is obvious, the natural resource base in the country is shrinking. There are also signs of degradation of land and overexploitation of water in the country. This throws the second biggest challenge to ensure sustainable use of natural resources.

The post-WTO period has thrown serious challenges to Indian agriculture, as domestic prices of several commodities have risen above international prices. This has made imports attractive and adversely affected exports. The situation calls for improving competitiveness of Indian agriculture which requires improvement in efficiency in agricultural production, marketing, transport and so on. This is the third challenge facing Indian agriculture.

Then come equity concerns with respect to sectors, regions, classes of farmers and gender. There is a strong feeling that intervention in food markets has benefited only the agriculturally progressive regions and rainfed and dryland agriculture and regions have been ignored. There is also serious concern about the viability and future of smaller-size holdings which constitute the majority of farmers in the country.

The present dismal picture of agriculture has resulted from several factors/reasons. The foremost is the lack of a clear policy on agriculture. The country has not changed institutional mechanisms and the regulatory framework to create an environment conducive to agricultural growth which was needed to adjust to changes in the domestic and global environment. This relates particularly to participation by the private sector in output markets and seed market. The second reason is a neglect of infrastructure and diversion of resources to populist measures. A third reason is a slowdown in technology reaching regions that need it, and a weakening of the extension system for dissemination of technology. Unless drastic reforms are implemented in the agriculture sector it will not be possible to revive output growth on a sustainable basis and mitigate rural distress.

Against this backdrop the chapter examines the severity of various challenges facing India's agriculture sector and how it would impact on overall growth of the Indian economy. The chapter is organized into five sections: the first section provides a historical perspective of agricultural policies followed in the country and the context for these policies; the second section analyses growth rates in Indian agriculture in different periods and presents the recent picture of growth in different sub-sectors of agriculture. The third to fifth sections discuss issues related to other challenges concerning equity, sustainability and efficiency, while reasons for the dismal growth scenario and emergence of other challenges are discussed in the sixth section. A final section examines implications of different growth scenarios in the agriculture sector for growth of the Indian economy.

Agricultural policy framework

In terms of agricultural development and policies the post Independence period can be divided into four distinct phases. The first phase covers the period up to the early 1960s and is termed the pre-green period. This period was marked by large-scale agrarian reforms, institutional changes and development of major irrigation projects. Intermediary landlordism was abolished, tenant operators were given security of farming and ownership of land. Land-ceiling acts were imposed by all the states to eliminate large-sized holdings, and cooperative credit institutions were strengthened to check the exploitation of cultivators by private money-lenders and traders. Land consolidation was also affected to reduce the number of land fragments and to provide land to landowners at one place in the same village as far as possible.

Expansion of cultivated area was the main source of growth in the pre-green revolution period, but this did not result in sufficient growth rate in agriculture to meet the food needs of the country. India faced a severe food shortage crisis in the early 1960s for which large imports of wheat had to be made. This forced the policy-makers to realize that in future continuous reliance on food imports and aid would impose heavy costs in terms of political pressure and economic instability (Rao, 1996). There was a desperate search for a quick breakthrough in agricultural production. One choice before the country was to introduce into cultivation new seeds of high yielding varieties (HYV) of wheat and rice which were available through the Consultative Group on International Agricultural Research (CGIAR) institutes like the Centro Internacional de Mejoramiento de Maíze y Trigo (CIMMYT) (International Maize and Wheat Improvement Centre) and the International Rice Research Institute (IRRI). Amidst a serious debate the government took a bold decision then to import and spread the HYV of wheat and rice which required the use of fertilizers and irrigation. This marked the second phase in the agriculture policy of the country. The strategy produced quick results as there was a quantum leap in yield. Consequently, wheat and rice production over a short span of six years between 1965–66 and 1971–72 witnessed an increase of 30 million tonnes which is 168 per cent higher than the total achievement in the 15 years following 1950–51.

The scope for area expansion diminished considerably in the green-revolution period in which the growth rate in area was less than half the growth rate in the first period. Increases in productivity became the main source of growth in crop output and there was a significant acceleration in yield growth in the green-revolution period. The main source of productivity increase was technological breakthrough in wheat and rice.

The new agricultural strategy, also known as the green-revolution technology, had its greatest success in the attainment of self-sufficiency in foodgrains. As the technology involved the use of modern farm inputs, its spread led to a fast growth in the agro-input industry. Agrarian reforms during this period took a back seat while research, extension, input supply, credit, marketing, price support and spread of technology were the prime concern of policy-makers (Rao, 1996).

Two very important institutions, namely, the Food Corporation of India and the Agricultural Prices Commission (subsequently renamed as the Commission for Agricultural Costs and Prices), were created at the beginning of green-revolution period to ensure remunerative prices to producers, to maintain reasonable prices for consumers, and to maintain a buffer stock to guard against the adverse impact of year-to-year fluctuations in output on price stability. These two institutions have mainly benefited rice and wheat crops which are the major cereals and staple food for the country (Chand, 2005a).

The next phase in Indian agriculture began in the early 1980s. Agricultural growth accompanied by an increase in real farm incomes led to the emergence of interest groups and lobbies which started influencing the farm policy in the country. There has been a considerable increase in subsidies and support to the agriculture sector during this period while public sector spending in agriculture for infrastructure development started showing a decline in real terms but investments by farmers kept moving on a rising trend (Mishra and Chand, 1995; Chand, 2001). The output growth, which was concentrated in very narrow pockets, became somewhat broad-based and gained momentum. The rural economy started witnessing a process of diversification which led to a growth in non-foodgrain outputs like milk, fishery products, poultry, vegetables, fruits, and so on. This accelerated a largely market-driven growth in agricultural GDP which continued up to the initial years of the 1990s. This period is termed as the period of wider dissemination of technology.

The decade of the 1980s did not see any major policy initiative for agriculture; the wider spread of improved technology was the main factor for output growth. Towards the late 1980s, some adverse consequences of the new technology started to emerge when some pockets of the green-revolution areas started to show signs of strain on natural resources like land and water. The mounting burden of subsidies also put pressure on fiscal resources, and after 1980–81 public investment in agriculture started declining.

A new phase in India's economic policy started in 1991 that marked a significant departure from the past. The country initiated economic reforms in 1991, which involved deregulation, reduced government participation in economic activities, and liberalization. Though much of the reforms were not initiated in agriculture, the sector was affected indirectly by devaluation of the exchange rate, liberalization of external trade and disprotection to industry. Then came a new international trade accord and the WTO, requiring opening up of domestic market. Initially there were strong apprehensions about the impact of trade liberalization on Indian agriculture, which later turned out to be a real threat for several commodities produced in the country. The policies followed in the post-reform period affected agriculture primarily through improvements in terms of trade (ToT), driven mainly by substantial price hikes of paddy and wheat through government intervention. As government intervention in prices of wheat and paddy is confined to a limited producing area, the improvement in ToT did not benefit a large segment of agriculture. Other than price intervention there was no major policy initiative in agriculture till recently and the period has been marked by a sort of policy vacuum. It is pertinent to mention that in other sectors domestic liberalization and reforms either preceded or accompanied external liberalization. However, in the case of agriculture, the sequence of reforms was the reverse – external liberalization preceded internal liberalization and domestic reforms. The consequences have been (1) Indian agriculture was not able to take much advantage of post-WTO global liberalization, (2) an inability to compete with imports, and (3) a slowdown in agriculture growth. The most painful aspect of the state of farming during the reform period has been widespread rural distress and a spurt in the number of farmers committing suicide under economic duress.

Because of several adverse effects on agriculture seen during the reforms period there was a strong pressure on the government to come out with a formal statement of agriculture policy to provide a new direction to agriculture in the new and emerging scenario. In response to this, the government announced its New Agricultural Policy in July 2000, that aims to attain over the next two decades a growth rate in excess of 4 per cent per annum in agriculture. The policy lays down a number of other goals to attain this growth:

- the growth should be based on efficient use of resources and conserve India's soil, water and biodiversity;
- the growth should be with equity, that is growth which is widespread across regions and farmers;
- the growth should be demand-driven and cater to domestic markets, maximizing benefits from exports of agricultural products in the face of challenges arising from economic liberalization and globalization; and
- the growth must be sustainable technologically, environmentally and economically.

It is further reiterated that the policy will seek to promote technically sound, economically viable, environmentally non-degrading and socially acceptable use of the country's natural resources – land, water and genetic endowments to promote sustainable development of agriculture. These goals look to be quite ambitious at this juncture.

The document on National Agricultural Policy (NAP) released by the Government of India in July 2000 contains a set of policy intentions of the government. In order to implement those intentions a concrete and time-bound action plan was needed, but that is missing. The document is quite comprehensive in expressing what ought to be done in agriculture, and this is a first step in giving policy direction, but the subsequent step is how and when policy goals and objectives would be achieved. In most of the cases the NAP is silent on this, nor does it provide any follow-up document so that in more than three and half years no serious action has yet been initiated on most of these aspects.

Only recently has central government initiated some measures to effect domestic reforms in agriculture to change the regulatory and institutional environment and for increasing participation of the private sector in agriculture. These reforms include changes in the provisions of the Essential Commodities Act (1955), the Forward Contract (Regulation) Act (1952), and the Agricultural Produce Market Act (dates varying from state to state) at state level and removal of restrictions on inter-state movement of farm produce. These changes are expected to show their impact after some time, but since agriculture is of importance across states it is necessary to ensure that these reforms are not diluted at state level during their implementation.

Growth rates in agriculture: past and present

Indian agriculture depends heavily on vagaries of nature, particularly on the amount and distribution of rainfall as more than 60 per cent of the area under cultivation does not have access to irrigation. Consequently there are wide yearly fluctuations in total output and in annual rates of growth based on such output. In order to have a better understanding of growth trends in output, it was considered desirable to smooth the output series, and this was done by estimating growth rates based on a five-yearly (quinquennium) moving average of output. These growth rates are presented in Figure 6.1, that shows that growth in agricultural output witnessed a somewhat decelerating trend in the initial years after Independence and the output growth turned negative in the mid-1960s. The country then decided to adopt high yielding varieties of cereals, first of wheat and then paddy, which helped in reversing the declining growth trend. Output growth improved considerable around the late 1960s, but in the early 1970s there was a setback to growth due to the oil crisis. Again in 1979–80 India faced very severe drought which caused a dip in agricultural output. After that agricultural output followed an accelerated

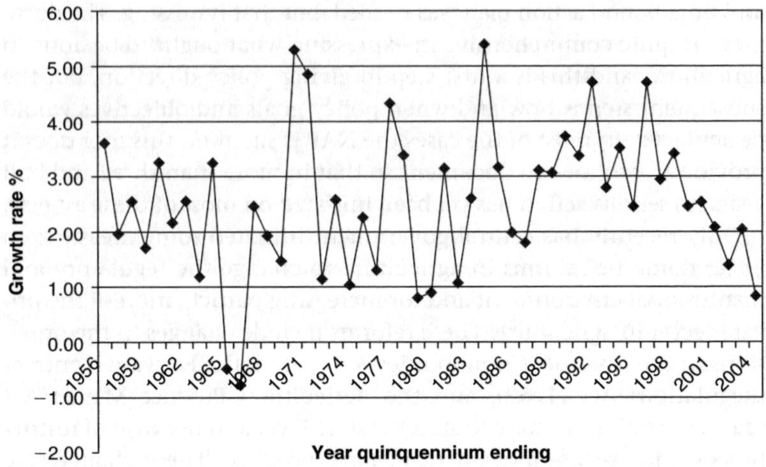

Figure 6.1 Annual growth-rate in GDP agriculture based on 5-yearly moving average series: 1956–2004

Table 6.1 Growth rate in GDP agriculture and non-agriculture sectors in different periods, per cent/year

Period	*Total economy*	*Non-agriculture*	*Agriculture*
I Pre-green revolution 1950/51–1964/65	3.95	5.59	2.66
II Green revolution period 1965/66–1979/80	3.62	4.40	2.76
III Wider technology dissemination period 1980/81–1994/95	5.37	6.56	3.33
IV Post reforms 1995/96–2003/04	5.69	6.95	1.86

Source: Government of India, *National Accounts Statistics*, New Delhi, various issues.

growth trend till 1994–95, where it peaked, subsequently, following a declining path up to the present. Over the last 50 years there has not been such a deceleration in growth of agricultural output as has been seen after 1994–95.

The series on growth trends indicate that phases of growth coincided with different phases of agricultural policy (Table 6.1). In the

Table 6.2 Growth rates (%) in output, input and value added in agriculture since 1950–51 at 1993–94 prices

Period	*Output*	*Input*	*Value added/farm income*
I Pre-green revolution 1950/51–1964/65	2.51	2.00	2.62
II Green revolution period 1965/66–1979/80	2.80	3.14	2.72
III Wider technology dissemination 1980/81–1994/95	3.22	2.64	3.38
IV Post reforms 1995/96–2003/04	1.69	1.84	1.65

Source: See Table 6.1.

pre-green revolution period the growth remained lowest even though lot of expansion in the area took place. Adoption of high-yielding varieties during late 1960s led to substantial increases in productivity of two principal crops grown in India, namely wheat and paddy, which raised output growth to 2.76 per cent during the 15 years following the green revolution. However, the adoption of green-revolution technology during this period remained concentrated in the north-west plains and some areas in southern India, both of which had assured water supplies for irrigation. Around 1980–81, improved technology spread to several other regions and the agricultural economy diversified; this resulted in a further acceleration in growth of agricultural output. This period also witnessed a sharp acceleration in the growth rate of the non-agriculture sector. After the mid-1990s the growth rate in agricultural output declined sharply.

Agricultural incomes, as measured by value added output, showed a similar pattern to GDP agriculture. This can be seen from growth rates in output, inputs and farm income presented in Table 6.2 pertaining to different sub-periods. In the pre-green-revolution period agricultural output increased annually by 2.51 per cent and the use of inputs increased at the rate of 2 per cent. Farm incomes in this period increased by 2.62 per cent a year. Adoption of green-revolution technology raised the use of inputs which accelerated growth in output to 2.80 per cent, and farm incomes in this period increased at a somewhat higher rate than the pre-green-revolution period. During 1980–81 to 1994–95 output growth further accelerated to 3.22 per cent despite

Table 6.3 Level and growth in per worker farm income at 1993–94 prices

Period	*Agricultural income per worker (Rs)*	*Growth rate in income in previous 10 years (%/year)*
1969/70–1973/74	9,049	
1979/80–1983/84	9,699	0.696
1989/90–1993/94	10,902	1.176
1999/00–2003/04	11,223	0.291

Source: See Table 6.1; and Government of India, *Agricultural Statistics at a Glance*, New Delhi.

a slowdown in the growth of input use. The net result has been a sharp growth in farm income which increased annually by 3.38 per cent. After 1994–95 the growth in use of inputs in agriculture plummeted to below 2 per cent which also brought down growth in output to about half of that seen during 1980–81 to 1994–95. The growth rate in farm income during the recent decade declined to 1.65 per cent per annum which is much lower than the growth during the previous five decades. This slowdown in farm income has serious implication for the livelihoods of those who are dependent on agriculture. If this slowdown in farm income has been accompanied by a shift in the workforce from agriculture to non-agriculture then the impact on the population dependent on agriculture would have been much less, but during this period the shift in the workforce from agriculture to non-agriculture has been very small and the population dependent on agricultural has been increasing.

A more precise picture of the slowdown in farm income can be obtained by looking at the level and growth of farm income per agriculture worker presented in Table 6.3. This is computed based on net farm income during the five years centred on 1971, 1981, 1991 and 2001 for which census estimates of agricultural workers are available. During the 1970s per worker farm income increased annually by 0.7 per cent; the growth rate accelerated to 1.18 per cent during the 1980s; and during the last decade farm income per worker increased by only 0.29 per cent.

Efficiency

Efficiency was not a serious issue in Indian agriculture until recently for three reasons. First, as there was a scarcity of food in the country the policies encouraged increases in production rather than reducing the average costs of production. Second, adoption of new technology, which resulted in an upward shift in production, involved a reduction in the average cost of production without putting any special emphasis on efficiency. Third, the agriculture sector was by and large insulated from competition from abroad through strict regulations on imports.

With liberalization, the issue of efficiency has become highly relevant as domestic production has to compete with products of other countries. In recent years domestic prices of several agricultural commodities have risen above international prices, and India is not able to check imports of a large number of commodities even at high tariffs. This is true not only in the case of imports from developed countries where agriculture is highly subsidized, but also in the case of products from developing countries. India is facing an import threat in the case of items like palm oil from Malaysia and Indonesia, spices from Vietnam, China and Indonesia, tea from Sri Lanka and rice from Thailand and Vietnam. This raises the question as to why most of the commodities produced in India cannot compete with produce from the international market. Is it due to low efficiency in production, or due to some other reasons?

Efficiency in trade involves efficiency at the level of production, marketing, processing, transport and so on. Farmers in India are at a considerable disadvantage compared to developed countries in respect of storage, marketing, processing, transport and post-harvest infrastructure. For several commodities, the transport cost from surplus to deficit states is much higher than freight from other countries to India (Chand, 2002). Similarly, domestic regulations and statutory charges add heavily to domestic prices and need to be rationalized. A study of India's edible oil sector by the World Bank (1997) brings out that India is indeed an efficient producer of important edible oil seeds, but it loses to other countries in prices of edible oil. The reason for this seems to be the high cost of oil seed processing and extraction, which in turn are related to low capacity utilization and lack of modern technology for oil seed processing. The average utilization rate of oil seed processing is only 30 per cent, wastage is high and the extraction rate is poor. All these factors combine to raise the price of domestically produced edible oil above the price of international markets, even though the cost of producing edible oil seeds is not higher in the country. Similar inefficiencies may be seen for other commodities. To compete with global produce, the country needs to reduce various post-harvest costs and undertake suitable reforms to improve the efficiency of domestic markets and the delivery system.

Another study based on a comparison of cost of production per unit of output between India and the USA shows that operating costs of Indian farmers in wheat, soyabean and cotton production is lower than for US farmers (Sen and Bhatia, 2004). Obviously, this implies that reasons for higher market prices in India could be either due to differences in post-harvest costs, or due to subsidies in some cases.

International prices for most of the agricultural commodities are moving on a downward trend in real terms. This suggests that to compete in a liberalized environment domestic prices must follow a similar trend, but this is not possible without technological breakthroughs or reductions in costs of production through crop shifts to move efficient regions. Some countries have very effectively applied biotechnology tools to raise yields, reduce costs of production, and improve the quality of some edible oil seeds which has given them significant advantage (see Phillips and Khachatourians, 2001). But India continues to suffer significant yield and production losses due to various biotic and abiotic stresses in oil seed and pulses. Biotechnology can help us understand tolerance mechanisms of plants to various stresses, identify gene(s) responsible for tolerance and transfer of genes for developing tolerant varieties. There are also reports of large areas being brought under transgenic crops namely soyabean, cotton and vegetables in countries like the USA, Argentina, Canada and China. It is estimated that, globally, transgenics were commercially grown on 44 million hectares (Qaim, 2001) and unconfirmed estimates indicate this area reached 80 million hectares by 2004–05. The immediate benefits of success of transgenics is a reduction in cost of production. However, these technologies are alleged to involve environmental and health risks and the Government of India has asked for trials on these crops for some more years. Some experts claim that transgenic crops and genetically modified foods can play a crucial role in raising the quantity and quality to address future demands and food security in India (Pental, 2005), while others question the suitability of such technologies for a developing country like India. They feel that traditional germplasm and conventional methods of breeding are far superior to the GM (genetically modified) approach to improve nutrition quality and to enhance productivity of various crops, and indicate that GM technology is expensive and full of hazards which cannot be checked by the weak regulatory systems prevailing in developing countries (Sahai, 2005).

While safety is a major concern for India in adopting transgenic crops, other countries producing such crops gain advantage over Indian production. The delay in safe adoption of these new technologies is making Indian produce less efficient relative to that of other countries.

Equity

Equity in India is generally considered in terms of sectoral, regional and gender aspects. Sectoral inequity can be seen from the growth rates in non-agricultural and agricultural sectors and the trends in per worker income in agriculture and non-agriculture. Annual rates of growth in GDP agriculture and non-agriculture based on five-yearly moving average series beginning with 1984–85 are presented in Figure 6.2. The two series of growth rate show that up to the early 1990s, the growth rate in the agriculture sector was accelerating and the difference in growth rates in the two series narrowed. After mid-1990s the growth rate in agriculture decelerated very sharply whereas the non-agriculture sector witnessed growth around 7 per cent. This created a large gap in the performance of the two sectors.

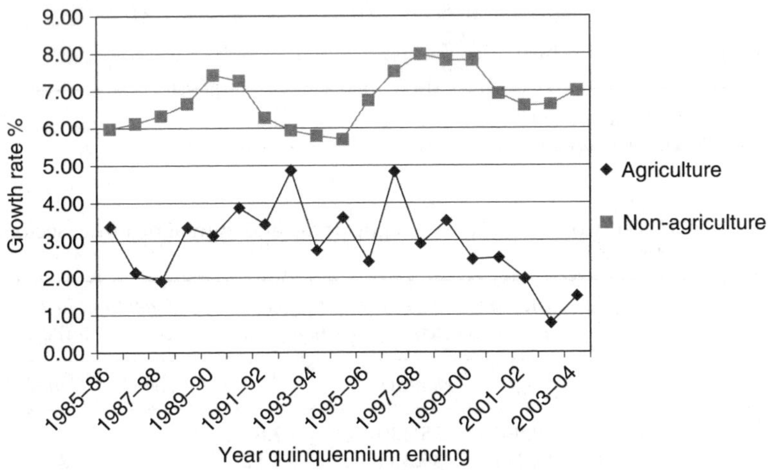

Figure 6.2 Growth rate in GDP agriculture and non-agriculture

The faster growth in output of the non-agriculture sector did not help much in shifting the workforce from agriculture to non-agriculture. Between 1980–81 and 2000–01 the share of agriculture in national income declined from 38.8 per cent to 25.4 per cent. The workforce engaged in agriculture in the same period witnessed a very small decline, from 60.5 per cent to 58.4 per cent (Table 6.4). The slow growth in agriculture with no significant decline in the labour force has created a serious disparity between agriculture and non-agriculture and urban and rural India. The magnitude of this can be seen from per worker income in agriculture and non-agriculture presented in Table 6.5. During the two decades after 1980–81, per worker income in the non-agriculture sector more than doubled whereas in agriculture this increase is less than 12 per cent. As a consequence, one worker in the non-agriculture sector earns more than the income of five workers in agriculture. This disparity is causing a lot of concern in the country and the rural vs urban or agricultural vs non-agricultural parts of the country are sometimes described as 'India v. Bharat', the former belonging to

Table 6.4 Share of agriculture in the economy's total output and employment

Year	*Share in NDP* at current price (%)*	*Share in employment (%)*
1980–81	38.8	60.5
1990–91	33.2	59.0
2000–01	25.5	58.4

*Net Domestic Product.
Source: See Tables 6.1 and 6.3.

Table 6.5 Per worker income in agriculture and non-agriculture sectors at 1993–94 prices

Period	*Income per worker (Rs)*		*Ratio of non-agri. to agri. income*	*Growth in last decade (%/year)*	
	Agri.	*Non-agri.*		*Agri.*	*Non-agri.*
1978/9 to 1983/4	9,961	28,430	2.85		
1988/9 to 1993/4	11,179	39,355	3.52	1.16	3.31
1998/9 to 2003/4	11,496	59,961	5.22	0.28	4.30

Source: See Tables 6.1 and 6.3.

the elite whose prosperity is growing and the latter belonging to commoners whose condition is not improving or is worsening.

The second aspect of disparity is interregional. Some regions of the country are agriculturally well-developed and have successfully experienced socioeconomic transformations through improvements in agricultural productivity and growth. However, agriculture in several regions remains backward, with low productivity and poor growth. The extent of regional variations in the agriculture sector can be seen from Figure 6.3 which shows variations in the value of agricultural output per hectare of cultivated area in early 1980 and around 2000. At current prices the coefficient of variation in per hectare value of crop output was 0.397 during 1988–89 which further increased to 0.46 during 1989–90.

A third aspect of inequity relates to gender rights in land. A large number of agricultural holdings are managed by women farmers, but empowering these women through rights in land has been a very difficult proposition as it involves changes in legislation in different states of the country, as agriculture is a state subject, and in most cases the consent of other family members particularly the male members. This not only affects the status of women in society, but also affects their access to technology and institutional credit. Some scholars suggest that a much easier way to strengthen women's rights in land is that land records show cultivation under women's names where they actually manage the farm (Chand, 2005b). This does not involve

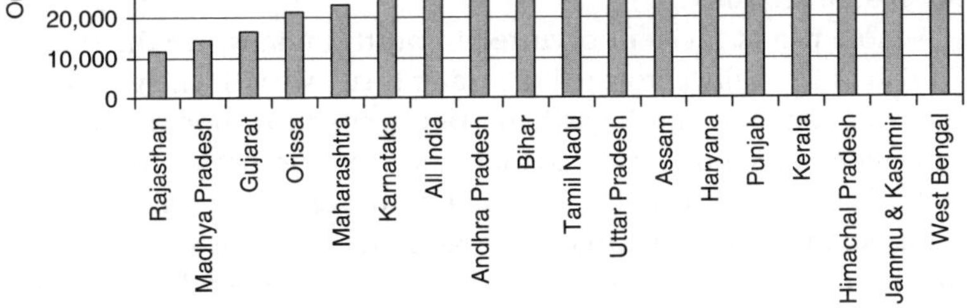

Figure 6.3 Regional variations in crop output per hectare of cultivated area during 2002–03

complications involved in transferring property rights but gives recognition to women in terms of title to cultivation. As information about the crop cultivated on each field and the name of the cultivator is recorded each season, it would be very easy to recognize women's status as farmers in this way. This could be achieved by instructing revenue officials to follow the factual position regarding the cultivation title. Subsequently, this should be supported by recognition of women as farmers for availing of all facilities like credit, and so on. Similarly, while undertaking the distribution of surplus land/wasteland the title should recognize the rights of males as well as females.

Sustainability

Sustainable use and management of water and land resources are important agro-environment issues in India. India has only 4 per cent of world water resources as against a 16 per cent share in world population, and water scarcity is more acute in the country compared to the world average. The demand for water is rising rapidly for non-agricultural uses as well as agricultural uses, but the more serious conflict is seen in the case of water use in agriculture. For groundwater this conflict is reflected in present vs future use of water, and in the case of surface water (river water) the conflict is seen in interstate water disputes over sharing of river water. The conflict between two southern states, Karnataka and Tamil Nadu, over the sharing of water from the river Cauvery is a classic case of a future scenario of water conflicts in India. Almost every year these states witness tensions, strikes and *bandh* (closedown) relating to distribution of Cauvery water. This has created lot of tension among the people of these two neighbouring states and some people have lost their lives in the agitations over water. All political and legal efforts have so far failed to resolve this conflict.

A more recent incident occurred in north India where the state of Punjab unilaterally abrogated the water treaty with the neighbouring states of Haryana and Rajasthan, and declined to honour the past agreement to supply water to Haryana into the newly constructed Satluj-Yamuna link canal where millions of rupees have already been invested. Farmers in Rajasthan have resorted to demonstrations against the short supply of canal water where again some farmers have lost their lives. These kinds of incidents are expected to increase in future.

The previous government headed by the Prime Minister Atal Behari Vajpayee launched a very ambitious project for interlinking rivers to take water from surplus to deficit rivers as a medium to long-term solution to mitigate the stress on water resources.

There is also a serious conflict around development of irrigation through multipurpose hydroelectric dams. Such projects are strongly opposed by environmentalists and those who are displaced due to submergence under dam water. The Sardar Sarovar project on the Narmada river in Madhya Pradesh could not be completed for several years because of such resistance. Finally, it was the verdict of the Supreme (Apex) Court which helped in completing this project. Prolonged delays in the construction of the Tehri Dam in Uttaranchal is another example of resistance by environmentalists and locals to such projects.

According to some scholars, the availability of ground water for irrigation will emerge as a critical bottleneck for self-sufficiency in foodgrains by the year 2020, as demand for irrigation will exceed its availability by nearly 30 per cent (Chopra and Golder, 2000). Similarly, the National Commission for Integrated Water Resource Development Plan has projected that the requirement for irrigation water in India will grow by more than 50 per cent by 2050. Based on various assessments it is concluded that even after fully exploiting available water resources, water suppliers can match the demand only if there is a big improvement in efficiency of irrigation.

Evidence is accumulating that the water table in several states is becoming depleted at a fast rate. In some areas of north-west India the water table is being lowered, and in some hard rock areas of peninsular India overexploitation of water has led to mining of water from deeper and deeper aquifers, ultimately leading to borewell failure. Previously in this area farmers had found cultivation of commercial crops very profitable and started expanding irrigation using pumpsets and borewells. As the hydrological factors were not favourable for recharging groundwater in the area the farmers driven by profit motive dug deeper borewells to exploit water in layers deeper than 800 feet. But even the deeper borewells did not last long. These heavy investments, incurred under debt, have not only ruined groundwater but also devastatated farmers in the region. Forced by distress, hundreds of farmers have been driven to commit suicide. This is best illustrated in the story of Musapally village (available on net at: www.indiatogether.org/2004/jun/psa-sinkbore.htm) which has more borewells than people.

This village in the district of Nalgonda in Andhra Pradesh has over 6,000 borewells for 2,000 acres of land under cultivation. Over 85 per cent of the borewells have failed and the rest are in decline. The desperate search for water is reported to have bankrupted this once prosperous village.

Even in the Indo-Gangetic region which was known to have adequate water resources for providing assured irrigation, and where shallow tubewells have brought a green revolution, farmers have started digging borewells at depths exceeding 500 feet as the groundwater in upper aquifers is depleting.

Some well-documented overt signs of groundwater overexploitation are:

- reductions in irrigated area per well;
- reductions in discharge of water from pumps and wells;
- increases in well-deepening by farmers; and
- premature drying up of shallow wells.

While demand for water is rising rapidly, the flow in rivers is declining. This is happening because of siltation in rivers and degradation of watersheds due to overgrazing, deforestation and increased human activities.

Among all natural resources, land is considered to be the worst affected natural resource in India. Land degradation takes place largely in the form of soil erosion due to water, which consists of direct erosion due to floods and surface run-off and indirect erosion due to excess or inappropriate use of water resulting in salinity and alkality. There is wide variation in various estimates of soil degradation, but those from the National Remote Sensing Agency (NRSA) are widedly accepted and are shown in Table 6.6.

These estimates show that degradation of land was rising rapidly in India. Comparable statistics for the 1980s show a more than 50 per cent increase in the area under degraded land in the short span of seven years between 1982 and 1989.

Floods are the major cause of land degradation. According to the Ministry of Agriculture, 40 million hectares in the country are prone to floods and on an average 8 million hectares of the total area and 3.70 million hectare of the gross cropped area is affected by flood.

Table 6.6 Extent of land degradation in India (millions of hectares)

Category	*1980–82*[1]	*1988–89*[1]	*1996–97*[2]
Salt affected	3.9	1.99	5.50
Waterlogged/marshy	0.88	1.22	8.53
Gullied/ravenous	4.33	2.02	3.97
With or without scrub	10.8	26.5	
Mining/industrial base		0.12	
Shifting cultivation	2.4	2.82	4.91
Degradad lands through special problems			29.52
Total degraded land	22.31	35.49	
as % of geographic area	6.79	10.8	
as % of cultivable area	11.31	18.0	

Sources: [1]National Remote Sensing Agency; [2]Ministry of Agriculture, Government of India, New Delhi.

Factors underlying agricultural challenges

The present challenges in Indian agriculture have resulted from cumulative effects over more than two decades. The underlying causes for these challenges relate to infrastructure, regulation, institutional factors and technology.

Infrastructure

Creation of infrastructure through public investment was considered crucial for long-term growth and development of the agriculture sector. The states have played a leading role in creating hardcore infrastructures like major and medium-sized irrigation projects, rural roads, rural electrification, setting up of agricultural markets. However, the beginning of the 1980s witnessed a very significant change in resource allocation policy to agriculture; it marked the beginning of a decline in public investment in agriculture and a sharp rise in subsidies provided to the sector.

After 1979–80, public investment in agriculture not only failed to keep pace with growth of GDP of the agriculture sector but their level also declined. In the early 1980s more than 4 per cent of GDP in agriculture was used in public investment. In recent years this has fallen to 1.54 per cent (Table 6.7 and Figure 6.4). The decline in public investment in agriculture is believed to be having an adverse impact on the creation of infrastructure in agriculture and on long-term growth of farm output.

Table 6.7 Public investment in agriculture at 1993–94 prices

Period	*Public investments (Rs. billions)*	*As % of GDP agriculture*
1980–84	70.33	4.08
1985–89	56.78	2.90
1990–94	48.44	2.07
1995–99	47.90	1.75
2000–02	45.65	1.54

Source: *National Accounts Statistics*, Central Statistical Organization, Government of India, various issues.

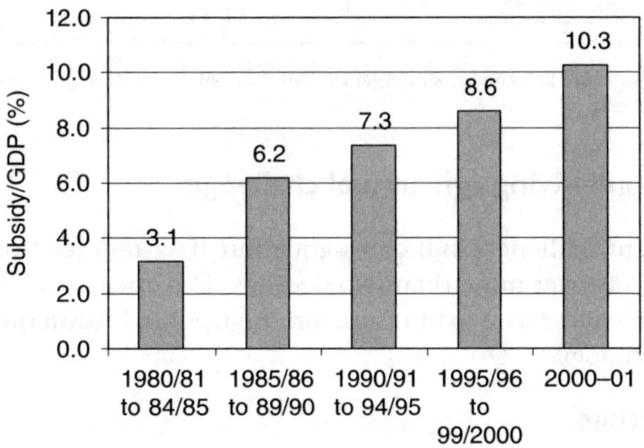

Figure 6.4 Input subsidies as % of GDP agriculture

In contrast to public investment, the level of subsidies provided on fertilizer, power and irrigation has increased more than five times in real terms since 1980. During the year 2000–01, India spent Rs.481 billion on subsidizing the three inputs. The share of subsidies in the GDP of agriculture was as small as 3.1 per cent during the first half of the 1980s, while in the second half of the 1980s it doubled to 6.2 per cent. The latest estimates reveal that subsidies now account for more than 10 per cent of the GDP of agriculture (Table 6.8 and Figure 6.5).

The decline in public investment has coincided with an increase in subsidies, and based on this some researchers feel that to meet the increase in current account expenditure (subsidy) the government has been forced to divert resources from the capital account (investment heads). Studies also show that the same amount of resources

Table 6.8 Subsidies in Indian agriculture

Period	*Total subsidies (Rs. billion/year)*		*Subsidies as share of GDP agriculture at current prices*
	Current price	*1993–94 prices*	
1980/81–84/85	20.8	54.6	3.1
1985/86–89/90	68.7	122.9	6.2
1990/91–94/95	157.5	171.8	7.3
1995/96–99/2000	339.5	236.1	8.6
2000–01	481.1	294.4	10.3

Sources: Data on fertilizer subsidies is taken from *Economic Survey*, Government of India, various issues; data on power and irrigation subsidies is from Gulati and Narayanan (2003).

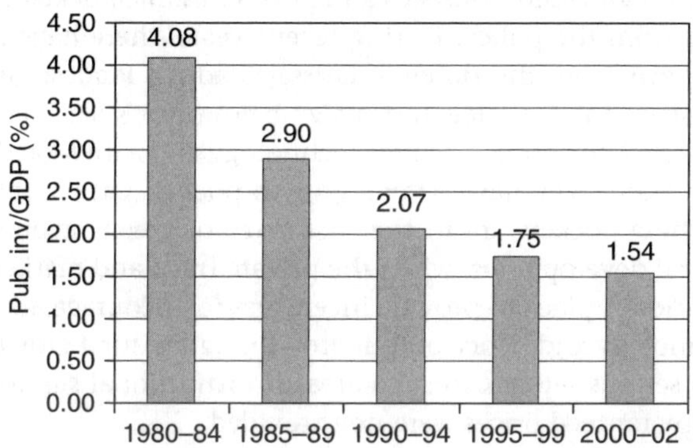

Figure 6.5 Public investment in agriculture as % of GDP agriculture

going into public investment gives a much higher return compared to the same resource going into subsidies (Chand and Kumar, 2004).

Agricultural price policy

India does not have a system of direct income support for agriculture. However, price support has been used as an instrument of ensuring remunerative prices for some crops under a system of minimum support prices for farm produce. Minimum support prices (MSP) serve as a surety to farmers that if the market price falls below the MSP or the guaranteed level, the government is under obligation to procure the produce offered for sale at the guaranteed price. Every season the government announces a minimum support price for paddy (rice), wheat, sorghum, pearl millet, finger millet, maize, ragi, barley, gram, pigeon pea, moong, urad, tur, rapeseed/mustard, toria, groundnut, sunflower, soybean, sesamum, nigerseed, cotton, jute, copra and tobacco. Sugarcane is covered under a statutory minimum price (SMP) – it is illegal for anybody to purchase sugarcane at less than its SMP.

Here it is pertinent to mention that the mere announcement of the MSP does not automatically guarantee that the market price would not fall below the MSP. Experience shows that institutional intervention in ensuring the guaranteed price is effective only in those regions and crops where government or public sector agencies procure the concerned commodities in a big way. Implementation of the MSP shows that rice and wheat are the main beneficiaries of the policy, while cotton and edible oilseeds and pulses in some pockets have also benefited from the policy. During recent years, there have been frequent reports from the states of Orissa, Madhya Pradesh and Bihar about distress sales of rice and maize below the MSP. These states, besides being late-adopters of new technology and with food deficits at aggregate state level, have several growth pockets with surplus foodgrains. These pockets are in the first stage of green revolution and agricultural development, when the private trade and market institutions are not in place to provide incentives to encourage adoption of new technology and hence output growth. Agricultural growth would receive a serious setback in such areas if institutional support in the form of guaranteed prices were not provided.

Government intervention in grain markets has come under much criticism due to its regional and commodity bias. Official procurement of foodgrains is alleged to be helping only a few states and concentrating their operations in already developed regions. States like Bihar, Gujarat, Madhya Pradesh, Karnataka and Maharashtra experienced sharp increases in marketed surpluses of wheat after 1983–84. Similarly, marketed surpluses of rice witnessed substantial increases in several states like Bihar, Gujarat, Karnataka, Kerala, Madhya Pradesh and Orissa. But farmers in these states have hardly benefited from government procurement policy. It is striking to observe that more than three-quarters of the wheat that arrived in markets in Punjab and Haryana was procured by official agencies, whereas only 2.2 per cent of marketed surplus in states other than Punjab, Haryana, Uttar Pradesh and Rajasthan was procured by official agencies (Table 6.9).

Table 6.9 Percent of market arrival of rice and wheat procured by official agencies in various states, average of 1994–95 to 1996–97

State	*Rice*	*Wheat*
Punjab	76.05	87.81
Haryana	59.17	75.61
Uttar Pradesh	20.15	18.04
Rajasthan		29.98
Andhra Pradesh	68.14	
Madhya Pradesh	27.42	
Orissa	35.99	
Tamil Nadu	15.60	
West Bengal	8.16	
Others	2.71	2.20
All India	39.70	49.94

Source: Government of India, *Food Statistics*, New Delhi, various issues.

Similarly, in the case of rice, more than three-quarters of market arrival in Punjab, 59 per cent in Haryana and 68 per cent in Andhra Pradesh was procured by official agencies. They purchased 8 to 37 per cent of rice brought to market in Madhya Pradesh, Orissa, Tamil Nadu and West Bengal. In other states, government procurement was below 3 per cent of market arrivals. This shows a very strong regional concentration of government intervention continuing in a selected few states.

This information shows that the main beneficiaries of wheat procurement have been Punjab and Haryana, and to some extent Uttar Pradesh and Rajasthan. In the case of the rice, the main beneficiaries have been Punjab, Andhra Pradesh and Haryana, while states like Uttar Pradesh, West Bengal, Orissa and Tamil Nadu have also benefited to some extent. The remaining states have hardly benefited from government procurement of grains even though these neglected states have shown a tremendous increase in generating marketing surpluses.

The system of incentive prices has remained confined to the regions which were early-adopters of green-revolution technology and are agriculturally well-developed. These regions have a strong infrastructure network where private trade and markets can function effectively. Productivity has approached a plateau and price incentives are not effective for further growth. On the other hand, large regions of the country are at a take-off stage of improved technology, but do not have well-developed markets and private trade is exploitative. Such regions require government intervention in terms of price support for some time to encourage adoption of improved technology with its large potential for growth in output.

Technology

India has a large network of research and technology that covers all agro-ecological pockets of the country. Institutes under the Indian Council of Agricultural Research, and the State Agricultural Universities claim to have varieties and technologies which are capable of giving high output per unit of resources. However, this has not helped in bridging the huge gap between what is attainable through these technologies and what is actually attained at farm-level in most of the crops and states. The reason could be that either the technologies having higher yield potential are not actually suitable at farm-level, or enough effort is not made to take the technologies from labs and experimental stations to farmers' fields. Technology policy needs to address the issue whether technologies are less appropriate or there is weakness in the technology-transferring extension systems.

Harnessing to benefits of technology requires well-developed systems for sales and distribution of seeds and plant propagation material. Till now the public sector has dominated the multiplication and supply of seed and plant propagation material, but it is highly inadequate to meet the emerging and growing needs and demand. There are also reports of some decay in the public distribution system of seeds, for several reasons, and advantage of this is being taken by unscrupulous private trade. However, there is a need to promote competition in the seed sector by encouraging large-scale private-sector participation in the seeds business.

Regulations

During the last decade and a half the economic and policy environment in India has undergone significant changes mainly due to new economic policy and economic reforms started in 1991, and domestic and global liberalization. This has raised new kinds of issues in agricultural markets and necessitated changes in existing regulations and systems. There is a strong concern that Indian agriculture has been subject to global competition through external liberalization without first going for internal liberalization.

Till recently, agricultural trade and marketing was subject to a plethora of central and state regulations like the Essential Commodities Act,

Restrictions on Free Movement of Agricultural Produce across states, the monopoly of Agricultural Market Committees on setting up of agricultural markets, and so on. These regulations have restricted competition and investments by private trade in agricultural markets, but were relevant to check hoarding and other exploitative practices when there were scarcities and markets were segmented. With the improved availability of various commodities and the development of communications and transport networks markets are becoming more spatially and temporally integrated. This environment is conducive for expanding business enterprise and promoting competition, which can be achieved by removing various obstacles in conducting business in agricultural produce which in turn would create a favourable economic environment for farm produce.

Only recently, central government has initiated some measures to effect domestic reforms in agriculture to change the regulatory and institutional environment and for increasing participation of the private sector in agriculture. These reforms include changes in the provisions of the Essential Commodities Act, the removal of restrictions on interstate movement of farm produce, the model Agricultural Produce Market Act, encouragement to contract farming, and the Forward Market Act. These changes are expected to show their impact after some time. However, agriculture being a state subject it is important to ensure that these reforms are not diluted at state level during their implementation.

Implications for growth of the economy

Based on its share in the total output of the economy, a 1 per cent increase in agriculture output pushes up the growth rate of the total economy by about 0.24 per cent. Conversely, a 1 per cent decline in agriculture output pulls down the growth rate of the total economy by 0.24 per cent. Second, due to strong forward and backward linkages with the rest of the economy the performance of agriculture causes significant effect on the growth rate of the non-agriculture sector, particularly in the case of industry. Recent empirical evidence suggests that a 1 per cent change in agriculture growth results in a 0.38 per cent change in the growth rate of industrial output (Bhanumurthy and Sinha, 2004). Thus, the growth rate of the agriculture sector is very important to meet India's quest to raise the

Table 6.10 Required growth rate in non-agricultural sector to achieve 8% and 10% growth rate in economy corresponding to various growth scenarios in agriculture sector

Scenario	*Growth rate (%/year)*			*Required growth in non-agri.*	
	Agri.	*Non-agri.*	*Total*	*For 8% growth rate*	*For 10% growth rate*
Historical	2.65	5.28	4.34	9.70	12.32
Recent	1.86	6.84	5.69	9.94	12.57
Planned	4.00		8.00	9.26	11.89
Further decline	1.00		10.00	10.21	12.84

growth rate of its economy first to an 8 per cent level and after a few years to 10 per cent.

Table 6.10 provides some ideas about growth rates needed in non-agriculture corresponding to different growth scenarios in agriculture to achieve different levels of overall growth in the economy.

The Indian economy during recent years has grown at a rate close to 6 per cent, and there is a strong feeling within the country and outside that this growth rate can be further accelerated. Official bodies in India have now set a goal of 8 per cent growth rate which is proposed to be raised to 10 per cent after a few years. Achieving an 8 per cent growth rate would required close to a 10 per cent growth in the non-agriculture sector corresponding to the recent growth rate in Indian agriculture. If, however, the agriculture growth rate decelerates to 1 per cent, which is probable if problems of agriculture are not addressed urgently and effectively, then the non-agriculture sector needs to increase by 10.2 per cent to achieve an 8 per cent overall growth rate, and by 12.84 per cent to achieve a growth rate of 10 per cent in the total economy. This growth rate in the non-agriculture sector would require a very sharp acceleration in the growth rate of the non-agriculture sector, which during the last decade has increased by 6.84 per cent annually.

Here it is pertinent to mention that there is vast potential in Indian agriculture and it is not so difficult to accelerate its growth rate. But this requires reforms in agriculture, the spread of new technology and some sort of price assurance to producers in the hitherto agriculturally lagging regions, particularly parts of east and central India.

References

Bhanumurthy, N.R. and S. Sinha (2004) 'Industrial Recovery: Can it be Sustained', *Economic and Political Weekly*, vol. 39, no. 5.

Chand R. (2001) 'Emerging Trends and Issues in Public and private Investments in Indian Agriculture: A Statewise Analysis', *Indian Journal. of Agricultural Economics*, vol. 56, no. 2, pp. 161–84.

— (2002) *Trade Liberalisation, WTO and Indian Agriculture: Experience and Prospects*. New Delhi: Mittal Publications, ch. 5.

— (2005a) 'Whither India's Food Policy: From Food Security to Food Deprivation', *Economic and Political Weekly*, vol. 40(12), pp. 1055–61.

— (2005b) 'India's National Agricultural Policy: A Critique', in R. Chand (ed.), *India's Agricultural Challenges, Reflections on Policy, Technology and other Issues*. New Delhi: Centre for Trade and Development, pp. 19–46.

Chand R. and P. Kumar (2004) 'Determinants of Capital Formation and Agriculture Growth: Some New Explorations', *Economic and Political Weekly*, vol. 39(52), pp. 5611–16.

Chopra K. and B. Goldar (2000) 'Sustainable Development Framework for India: The Case of Water Resources' (mimeo). Delhi: Institute of Economic Growth.

Gulati, A. and N. Sudha (2003) *The Subsidy Syndrome in Indian Agriculture*. New Delhi: Oxford University Press.

Mishra, S.N. and R. Chand (1995) 'Public and Private Capital Formation in Indian Agriculture: Comments on the Complementarity Hypothesis and Others', *Economic and Political Weekly*, Review of Agriculture, vol. 30.

Pental, D. (2005) 'Transgenic Crops for Indian Agriculture: An Assessment of their Relevance and Effective Use', in R. Chand (ed.), *India's Agricultural Challenges, Reflections on Policy, Technology and other Issues*. New Delhi: Centre for Trade and Development, pp. 129–60.

Phillips, P.W.D. and G.G. Khachatourians (2001) *The Biotechnology Revolution in Global Agriculture*: Innovation and Investment in the Canola Sector. Oxford: CABI Publishing.

Qaim M. (2001) 'Transgenic Crops and Developing Countries', *Economic and Political Weekly*, vol. 36(32), pp. 3064–70.

Rao V.M. (1996) 'Agricultural Development with a Human Face', *Economic and Political Weekly*, vol. 31(26), pp. A-50–A-62.

Sahai, S. (2005) 'Is AgBiotechnology Suited to Agricultural Production in India?', in R. Chand (ed.), *India's Agricultural Challenges, Reflections on Policy, Technology and other Issues*. New Delhi: Centre for Trade and Development, pp. 161–70.

Sen, A. and M.S. Bhatia (2004) *Cost of Production and Farm Income, Millennium Study on State of India's Farmers*. New Delhi: Academic Foundation.

World Bank (1997) *The Indian Oilseed Complex: Capturing Market Opportunities*, Vol. I and II, Report no. 15677-IN, 31 July.

7
Conclusion and Summary

This book has discussed the progress of economic integration in East Asia, and the expanding role played by India in that framework. In his concluding address to the December 2005 International Symposium, Dr Masahisa Fujita reiterated the view that India, though one of the 'Big Three' in Asia, was receiving less attention than China, both from Japan and globally. Nevertheless, Japanese multinational companies saw India as an essential link in the global value chain, particularly with regard to the automobile market and the investment of mutual funds. Concerning India's relationship with Japan via the automobile market, Suzuki and Honda accounted for over half of India's market in both cars and motorcycles. Regarding the investment of mutual funds from Japan to India, the managed assets in India had increased by a factor of 100 in the preceding year, reflecting the general public to view India's rise to prominence as that of a 'behemoth'.

Dr Fujita suggested that this global interest in India began in October 2003, with the publication of the Goldman Sachs paper 'Dreaming with BRICs: the path to 2050'. The paper argued that if the current status would continue, Chinese GDP would overtake that of Japan by 2015. Moreover, by the early 2030s, India's GDP would also surpass Japan's. Dr Fujita calls this a 'simplistic assumption', since progress would not follow a straight line in the real world. However, despite the inevitable 'ups and downs over the longer term', both China and India will be on course to grow into huge economic powers. He then drew a comparison with expectations in the 1960s of the economic success of the Soviet Union – which subsequently collapsed. Dr Fujita maintained that this could not happen in the case of India because it is a mature democracy with a well developed capitalist structure, and these conditions provided a good basis for sustained growth.

On the other hand, he pointed out, democracy could be experienced as restrictive. As he put it,

> for example, in China if someone decides to build a highway, then so be it. But that does not happen in India because there is democracy and individual property rights and you have to proceed according to law, so it takes time.

Over the long term, though, he said there would be

> three hegemons – Japan, China and India – as well as the four tigers, and that combined with ASEAN would really give East Asia a great presence in the global arena.

Dr Fujita felt that this would have a beneficial effect on both economic growth and international peace.

Professor Bhagwati, in his closing address, stated that he felt India and Japan were natural allies, since they were both democracies. He felt that Japan had long wanted to invest in India, but that India had not been keen on foreign investment. Now that was changing and India could be seen as a logical investment partner for Japan because the two countries had no direct involvement with each other during the Second World War and were therefore not hampered by memories of that time. War memories in countries such as Korea and China have given rise to complications in their economic relations with Japan. Also, from India's point of view, another point in Japan's favour is that it did not stand for 'the empire' like western countries did, so left-wing opinion would also be satisfied on that score concerning Japanese investment. Therefore there was scope for considerable expansion of trade and investment between the two countries.

Dr Homi Kharas, in his summing up, expressed his concerns about the long-term nature of foreign direct investment's role in India's economic integration with the rest of East Asia. He highlighted the difficulties involved in the movement of goods, not only because of infrastructural bottlenecks but because of bottlenecks caused by inefficient and complicated customs procedures at the points where goods have to cross borders. He cited this as a barrier to building up enough foreign investment to drive the process of integration in India, saying that this was regrettable because East Asia had a great deal of capital available to invest abroad. Dr Kharas suggested that integration would take place through financial markets rather than foreign investment, thus limiting the gains for both sides. He felt that there were two areas of maximum potential gain; the exportation of services, a field in which India is a global player, and Asian exportation of goods to India, which might well be expanding as a result of the interest created by India's aforementioned success in the services sector.

Dr Kharas also commented on the fact that Indian agriculture was not growing as rapidly as the rest of the economy. He described as one of the features of East Asian growth and poverty reduction, the fact that rural development more or less kept pace with the overall economic expansion, because even if people did not leave the rural areas, they moved from agricultural to non-agricultural production. This limited the gap which might otherwise occur between rural and urban incomes, so playing an important part in maintaining stability. Stability and security, Dr Kharas pointed out, are fundamental to the continuation of growth, and their attainment presents India with a significant challenge which it must address in order to benefit fully from opening up its economy.

Dr Zhang Yuyan remarked that, although India was the topic of the symposium, it had been mentioned less frequently than China. In China, however, academic and political discussions about India focused on the challenge presented by India and the impact it was likely to have on China in the future. Chinese scholars with an interest in India could, he said, be roughly divided into three groups. The first group regarded India as a rising, rather than a potential power. They respected India's achievements in the service sector, especially in IT and other high-tech industries. They were concerned about China's position in the international division of labour, and regarded China as a world assembly-line or workshop, rather than a world factory. India, on the other hand, they viewed as a world office and had mixed feelings about this position. In the eyes of these scholars, IT was a sort of service industry which would lead us to the future and China had lagged far behind India in this respect. They also attributed India's economic rise to its banking and financial systems, which they saw as healthier than China's, and to its relatively stable social environment in which 'a sizable middle class plays a critical role'. Dr Zhang went on to emphasize the point made by Dr Kharas regarding the necessity to remove the plethora of regulations and potentiality of faster economic growth after the removal of barriers and regulations. He pointed out that without such barriers India would have easy access to the world market because so many Indian people could speak fluent English (as demonstrated by the country's huge success in the IT industry).

According to Dr Zhang, the second group of India-focused Chinese scholars held a largely opposite view to those in the first group. This second group was either pessimistic or sceptical about India's long-term economic sustainability, some of the reasons for this view having been mentioned earlier, i.e. infrastructure problems, political opposition to further reform, obstacles created by vested interests and lobbies and the decline of agriculture. In addition to these problems, scholars in the second group cited lack of skills and education among the labour force as a reason for pessimism about India's long-term economic success. India was seen by this group as having a much higher illiteracy rate than that of China, people with fewer than four years of education accounting for about 40 per cent of India's labour force, and in this respect India had 'a long way to go to catch up with China, particularly regarding the labour force in the manufacturing industries'.

With reference to India's success in the IT industry, this second group maintained that no country in history had ever successfully industrialized its economy without a sizable and competitive manufacturing sector. In their opinion this meant that there was no need to worry about China's position in the international market being overtaken by India in the coming years. This view was later supported by Professor Bhagwati, who pointed out that the productivity of a country's investment depended on the productivity of the labour force and that India's lack of education would therefore reduce its productivity potential. He cited this as a great weakness which might give rise to disappointment in India's long-term hopes.

The third group of scholars was described by Dr Zhang as having a moderate view, seeing India as a potential economic power that presented both a challenge and an opportunity for China. There was room, they felt, for the two countries to benefit greatly from trade and cooperation with each other, the main obstacle being the regulations relating to trade and investment mentioned earlier. By the end of 2004, for example, China's investment in India was only one tenth of India's investment in China and the shortfall was considered to have been a result of the Indian government's intervention in the market. Dr Zhang then aligned his own views with those of the third group and advocated a 'good neighbours' approach to future trading operations. Like Dr Fujita, he had hopes for future prosperity in an Asia led by the 'Big Three'.

Chularat Suteethorn in her summing up highlighted some risks in fostering economic relations between Thailand and India. On the macroeconomic side the internal fiscal balance needed consideration, India's deficits being about 10 per cent of its GDP; a critical factor which could affect the stability of India's economy in the long run. In order to maintain a high growth rate, the government would have to promote steady investment and trade expansion and rein in unnecessary spending to keep inflation under control. A second risk was posed by the trade negotiations' 'rules of origin'. Ms. Suteethorn pointed out that, despite the existence of the FTA and tariff reduction, if exporters did not fulfil the rules by obtaining certificates of origin, they would be unable to benefit from the Free Trade Agreement. A third risk, she maintained, arose from the number of 'sensitive items' which both sides probably wished to keep outside the FTA. However, this arrangement had to operate within WTO rules that tariff reduction had substantially to cover all trade, meaning that sensitive items had to be kept to a minimum. The last point which Ms Suteethorn made was that custom tariff rates needed to be significantly reduced, and this would mean that loss of revenue would have to be considered. The governments of importing countries would have to pay a considerable amount of compensation to groups affected by this tariff reduction, and certain sectors which had enjoyed protection would also have to make adjustments in order to survive in the era of globalization.

In response to Dr Kharas' comments on the importance of the service sector and the capital market in Asia, Ms Suteethorn raised the matter of promoting the Asian Bond Markets in order to keep a lot of savings in Asia. She also highlighted the important part played by the ACD (Asia Cooperation Dialogue), which consists of 28 member countries currently. Thailand is a prime mover of Asian Bond Market Development Initiative in the ACD. Moreover, Executives' Meeting of East Asia and Pacific Central Banks has already set up Asian Bond Fund to promote Asian Bond Markets.

Dr Fujita commented further on the obstacles presented by the 'rule of origin' mentioned by Ms Suteethorn, saying it gave rise to a 'spaghetti bowl' effect whereby each small transaction added to the complications until the problem became so big that nothing could move. He said that there was now a great need for cooperation in arriving at a multilateral trade agreement.

Dr Uchikawa, in his summary, commended India for taking advantage of globalization. Rapid growth of IT industry and transfer technology from multinational companies are examples. However, he pointed out that globalization also created problems, one being that 'employment elasticity' declined. In agriculture, mechanization was proceeding. In manufacturing, if India were to compete with other countries, the latest technology must be utilized. In services, rationalization need to be implemented to improve competitiveness. As a result, growth rates of employment are less than those of value added. The IT industry was absorbing the labour force, but entry to the IT industry required a level of education which many Indian people did not have. The creation of employment opportunities was therefore a big issue in India, and one way forward was the rural development route. First there should be substantial investment in agriculture, which would enable the income of farmers to improve. This would give farmers greater spending power, and in turn might increase expenditure on services, causing that sector to grow in rural areas. Dr Uchiwaka argued that the WTO would be unable to reach an agreement regarding liberalization in developing countries if employment problems were neglected. Dr Fujita then commented on the importance of improving educational opportunities if these goals were to be realized.

In his summary, Dr Chand commented on the 34 per cent decline in agriculture's share of India's GDP over the past half-century and questioned why this had not been accompanied by a similar decline in agricultural employment. He questioned the wisdom of labour-market reforms which followed a capital-intensive rather than a labour-intensive route, when labour was so widely available, and advocated measures to shift this large labour force out of agriculture and into industry. He also called for the liberalization of regulations which still restricted agriculture, although they had been lifted in other areas of work.

In comparing India with China, Dr Chand outlined the important part played by nutrition of people. He stated that, despite economic growth, the average protein and calorie intake of the Indian population as a whole after 1991 had declined and that there was an increasingly high percentage of undernourished people. The phonomenon was explained by the fact that non-food need and influence of consumerism made an intentional choice to sacrifice on food in order to make a preference for non-food items. China, on the other hand, had addressed this problem and there had been an overall improvement in the nutrition of its population.

In conclusion, Dr Chand said that India and China had some good things to learn from each other, but there were dark as well as bright sides to the comparisons. Such comparisons should be seen, he said, as enriching both countries with better choices rather than as a cue to imitate each other exactly.

Before closing the symposium, Dr Fujita quoted a recent special edition of *The Economist* (21–27 February 2004), in which there was an article entitled 'India's Shining Hopes'. Describing the journal as being of 'modest or conservative opinion, Dr Fujita stated that 'even *The Economist* said that there are strong reasons to believe that India will repeat the really impressive and surprising growth of China ... in the middle and long run'. He then emphasized the importance of increasing and improving India's airline connections with the major cities of the world in order to facilitate this projected economic growth.

Index

Notes: f = figure; n = note; t = table; **bold** = extended discussion or heading emphasized in main text; 91[–]93 = proceed direct from page 91 to page 93.